WHY
ARE WE HERE?

WHY ARE WE HERE?

EVERYDAY QUESTIONS AND THE CHRISTIAN LIFE

EDITED BY

Ronald F. Thiemann

AND

William C. Placher

TRINITY PRESS INTERNATIONAL
Harrisburg, Pennsylvania

A study guide is available for this book on www.morehousegroup.com.

Cover art: Superstock, Man in the World by P. Filonov

Copyright © 1998 by Trinity Press International

Trinity Press International, P.O. Box 1321, Harrisburg, PA 17105
Trinity Press International is a division of the Morehouse Group

Library of Congress Cataloging-in-Publication Data

Why are we here? : everyday questions and the Christian life / edited
   by Ronald F. Thiemann and William C. Placher.
         p.   cm.
      Includes bibliographical references.
      ISBN 1-56338-236-9
      1. Theology, Doctrinal – Popular works.   I. Thiemann, Ronald F.
II. Placher, William C. (William Carl), 1948-   .
BT77.W485 1998
230 – DC21   97-49443

Printed in the United States of America

98   99   00   01   02   10   9   8   7   6   5   4   3   2   1

CONTENTS

CONTRIBUTORS

James J. Buckley is Professor of Theology at Loyola College in Maryland. He has published *Seeking the Humanity of God: Practices, Doctrines, and Catholic Theology* as well as articles in *Theological Studies, Heythrop Journal, The Thomist, Pro Ecclesia,* and *Modern Theology.* He is co-editor (with L. Gregory Jones) of *Modern Theology* as well as the Blackwell Readings in Modern Theology. He is currently working on a "Handbook of Ecclesiastical Opposition."

David Dawson is Associate Professor of Religion and Comparative Literature and Constance and Robert MacCrate Professor in Social Responsibility at Haverford College. He is the author of *Allegorical Readers and Cultural Revision in Ancient Alexandria* and *Literary Theory,* in the series Guides to Theological Inquiry.

J. A. Di Noia, O.P., is executive director of the Secretariat for Doctrine and Pastoral Practices of the National Conference of Catholic Bishops in Washington, D.C., Professor of Systematic Theology at the Dominican House of Studies, and editor-in-chief of *The Thomist.* His publications include *The Diversity of Religions: A Christian Perspective.*

George Hunsinger works at Princeton Theological Seminary as the director of its Center for Barth Studies. He is the author of *How to Read Karl Barth: The Shape of His Theology.*

Bruce D. Marshall is Professor of Religion at St. Olaf College. He is the author of the forthcoming *Trinity and Truth* and of *Christology in Conflict,* and the editor of *Theology and Dialogue: Essays in Conversation with George Lindbeck.*

William C. Placher chairs the department of philosophy and religion at Wabash College. His books include *A History of Christian Theology, Unapologetic Theology, Narratives of a Vulnerable God,* and *The Domestication of Transcendence.* He is an elder in the Presbyterian Church (USA) and has served on committees to draft the Presbyterian Church's Brief Statement of Faith and new catechisms.

Michael Root is Professor for Systematic Theology at Trinity Lutheran Seminary, Columbus, Ohio. Formerly Research Professor and director at the Institute for Ecumenical Research in Strasbourg, France, he is the author, with Gabriel Fackre, of *Affirmations and Admonitions* and editor of *Justification by Faith* (with Karl Lehmann and William Rusch) and *Baptism and the Unity of the Church* (with Risto Saarinen).

Kathryn Tanner is Associate Professor of Theology at the University of Chicago Divinity School. She is the author of three books: *God and Creation in Christian Theology; The Politics of God;* and *Theories of Culture: A New Agenda for Theology.*

Ronald F. Thiemann is Dean and John Lord O'Brian Professor of Divinity at Harvard Divinity School. He is the author of *Religion in Public Life: A Dilemma for Democracy, Constructing a Public Theology: The Church in a Pluralistic Culture,* and *Revelation and Theology: The Gospel as Narrated Promise.*

Thomas F. Tracy is Professor of Religion and Chair of the Department of Philosophy and Religion at Bates College. He has written *God, Action, and Embodiment* and edited *The God Who Acts: Philosophical and Theological Explorations* (Penn State, 1994), as well as authoring a variety of essays on divine action, the problem of evil, and the relations between theology and science.

William Werpehowski is Associate Professor of Theology and Religious Studies and associate director of the Center for Peace and Justice Education at Villanova University. He teaches and writes in the area of Christian ethics.

INTRODUCTION

William C. Placher

Christians don't just believe — we think about what we believe. After all, we have to explain our faith to our children, our skeptical friends, and the sometimes puzzled voices within each of us. We have to figure out what difference it makes to our politics, our careers, indeed every aspect of our lives. When our lives fall apart, we have to see whether or not our faith holds together. Therefore Christians — as well as the once-Christians, the not-quite-yet-Christians, and the clearly non-Christians — find ourselves thinking about Christian faith. Perhaps we join an adult discussion class at our church. Perhaps we rummage through the religion section of the local bookstore. We're not satisfied with simple answers.

Yet there are powerful forces in our culture that want to push us into simple answers. To some nonbelievers, *thoughtful Christian faith* seems a contradiction in terms. Religion in general, and sometimes Christianity in particular, strikes them as just silly on the face of it, obviously outmoded superstition. Thinking and believing don't go together since, if you really thought, you wouldn't believe.

Sometimes the loudest "Christian" voices don't seem very friendly to thoughtful Christian faith either. *Christian* has become a term for one party in American cultural politics. *Christian television*, *Christian candidates* — we know what such terms mean. They mean voting for Pat Buchanan or Pat Robertson, attacking homosexuality, favoring the death penalty. They imply impatience with argument and ambiguity. In a world of black and white, heroes and villains, there scarcely seems much need to think about one's faith — indeed, asking too many questions gets labeled as dangerous skepticism.

If, in defiance of these cultural forces, some people nevertheless want to think about their faith, where should they turn for help? *Theology* is the intellectual discipline that engages in thinking about faith. The authors of this book are all Christian theologians. That does not make us the ultimate experts in Christian faith. Out of prayer or suffering or lives of Christian love, many people without theological training probe closer to the center of what it means to believe and live as a Christian than most theologians. But still — we theologians have some training in the history and logic of Christian belief. If Christian faith itself really matters, then our particular expertise ought to give some helpful insights to our fellow Christians. We ought to be willing to offer that help when we can, as Christian theologians have done down through the centuries.

For the last generation or two, however, most theologians have been falling down on the job. We have too often stayed out of popular debates and written just for fellow scholars. We have our excuses. Our educations taught us the skills of scholarly research but often gave us little training in explaining what we have learned to a wider audience. Sometimes the popular debates seem so far removed from what we understand about the Christian tradition that we throw up our hands, not knowing where to begin. Sometimes the politics looks likely to get nasty. So, many of us teach our classes and write our articles for fellow specialists and stay out of the fights.

The needs of our time, however, are too urgent to tolerate such excuses. Christian faith offers both challenges and comforts that contemporary people need desperately to hear. Non-Christians need to encounter a form of Christian faith that demands their intellectual respect. Christians need help in putting together the pieces of their intellectual worlds. Even theologians struggle with the meaning of faith; we certainly do not have all the answers. But to the extent that our training gives us some help to offer, we owe it to our own vocations and to our neighbors' need to offer what we can.

A number of recent books and even television programs have reflected about Christian faith in a way accessible to a wide audience. This book represents another such effort. Its authors come from different points of view. Some are Catholics; some come from a range of Protestant traditions. One is a Dominican priest; several are ordained Protestant ministers; several are laypeople. We live in small towns and big cities in different parts of the country.

We happen to be friends. We went to the same graduate school (Yale) and had many of the same teachers. For nearly twenty years most of us have been meeting, with a few other friends, at least once a year to talk about our work and our lives. It's the depth of that ongoing friendship that makes a collaborative project like this possible. If our friendship makes the book possible, however, we did not write the book simply to celebrate that friendship. We have been thinking about Christian faith most of our lives. We want to share — with fellow Christians and curious bystanders alike — the intellectual and spiritual wealth and excitement and complexity we have found in that faith.

The essays that follow do not claim to answer every question, or even the most important ones. They offer at most some starting points, some examples of what it is like to think hard as a Christian about serious questions that really matter to people. For instance the first essay considers perhaps the most basic question of all: Why are we here? How should we understand the meaning of our lives? What purpose does the God of Christian faith have for us? Given how important these questions are, most of us strangely pay little attention to them, day in and day out. So the second essay turns to the question, Why are we so indifferent about our spiritual lives? We often do think most directly about our faith and our spiritual lives in the face of tragedy. It's when something goes badly wrong, when we encounter great suffering, that we think hardest about *why*. The third essay in this volume, therefore, considers more specifically the question, Why do the innocent suffer?

One of the assumptions we, the authors of this book, share is that a God worth thinking about can't be just a generic God, one to be addressed as "To Whom It May Concern." One needs to know something about the God in whom one believes and to whom one prays. Christian faith teaches about the particular God revealed in Jesus Christ. That conviction raises some important questions, which the next two essays address. Is Jesus

Christ the only way to salvation? That's a question of particular worry as many Christians know increasing numbers of non-Christians as our friends and neighbors. And — if Jesus Christ *is* the way to salvation, what are we to make of the current popular tendency to search for some other sort of connection with God through angels?

Belief in this God revealed in Christ ought to make a difference in the daily affairs of our lives. Christians ought to go to church. They ought to be disturbed that the Christian community is so deeply divided. Faith should affect what Christian parents teach their children and how Christian people think about their jobs. So a series of essays address these questions.

Whatever sense we make of our lives, however, if it all ends with our deaths, then the meaning and hope we have found are at the mercy of any cancer diagnosis, any terrorist's bomb, any random car accident. Christian faith therefore needs to look beyond death, as do the final two essays in this book: Must Christians believe in hell? Is there life after death?

What unites these varied essays, among other things, is a sense that Christian faith matters, that Christian faith isn't always easy to understand or to live, but that, beyond all puzzles and difficulties, it really does offer astonishing hope and amazing grace. As we were discussing this book, we talked a good bit about our intended audience. Were we writing for insiders or outsiders, for already committed Christians or curious bystanders? Rather to our surprise, we concluded that the answer to that question didn't much matter. Many outside the church are searching and studying about matters of faith; many inside the church (ourselves included!) still struggle with questions about what they believe and why. As several of these essays make clear, that struggle doesn't imply that we think getting involved in the church is unimportant — far from it! But it did turn out that if we were writing for seekers, for pilgrims still intellectually journeying in matters of faith, such folk are to be found both inside and outside Christian churches. Many centuries ago, Saint Augustine noted that our hearts are restless till they find their rest in God. This is a book for people who want to think more about Christian faith — it is, in other words, we hope, a book for those with restless hearts.

1

WHY ARE WE HERE?

Kathryn Tanner

Why are we here? is a question that reflective people of every time and place ask whenever some respite from the preoccupations of daily life offers them the chance to step back and assess the overall point of their lives, the meaning of it all. It is arguably a question with special urgency for people in the modern West, beset as we are by the worry that life holds no meaning beyond the immediate, partial, and fleeting achievements to be had in a world that disconcertingly often seems on the verge of running riot. Able to take nothing for granted in a time noted for its uncertainties, an age of irreducible diversity in orientations to life and of chastened pretensions to universal and unconditional truth, each of us takes on the responsibility for framing human life in terms that will give it some wider sense or import, some significance that exceeds the purely personal and that might persist despite the inevitability of disappointment and loss. Afforded the mixed blessings of life in the relatively stable and prosperous industrialized nations of the West, we do our jobs, lose our jobs, or retire; we struggle our lives through to eke out a comfortable existence in a competitive economy in which one person's gain always seems to come at another's loss; we raise our children and they leave home, or perhaps they die before us; we see our efforts to improve the world around us come to little; we run through, if we are lucky, a lifetime of petty entertainments; and then we ask, if we haven't already asked in anticipation or refusal of such ends to lives of constant occupation, What was the point? It is a question we each ask and answer for ourselves, with little help from the society at large, a society whose workings seem bent on nothing more than production and consumption according to purely functional norms such as efficiency and the maximization of profit.

If the threat of meaninglessness was not felt so keenly in prior centuries, Christian theologians have nevertheless always addressed the question at issue. Indeed, the whole of Christian theology — all the topics for discussion in Christian theology, from creation to salvation — provides a rich resource for contemporary people wrestling with the question of the wider import of their lives. If the pertinence of Christian theology to this question is not apparent, that is simply because the answers that Christianity offered were, in previous ages, there from the first as a kind of ready-made cultural currency, blunting the edge of worry that the question of meaning would otherwise pose for people left to their own devices, as they are in the more freewheeling cultural space of contemporary times. The question of meaning does not come through clearly in the history of Christian theology prior to the modern period simply because it is addressed so thoroughly from the first; the answer is offered before the question can even be asked.

But what sort of question is this? Modern circumstances may make the question more pointed and urgent by offering little help if and when the question arises, but in another way these same circumstances keep the question from becoming clearly visible at all. Modern times, in short, tend to make the question of meaning seem meaningless.

Who has the time for a question like that? What's the point? Better to be thoroughly engaged in the affairs of life, working hard, playing hard, immersed in what life has to offer people with the hope of making it in the modern West. Respite from practical worries, should one be fortunate enough to get it, is spent either in a state of exhaustion or in activities that are just as consuming of one's attention and energies. Reflection on the meaning of it all becomes a quixotic, almost quaint exercise, promising neither profit nor pleasure. In such a cultural climate, Christian theology is a worthless enterprise because the questions it answers are worthless.

Tranquilized or beaten down by the way life goes, by the endless run of things in modern times, we find ourselves stupefied by what is, sunk into the immediacy of things, in a way that atrophies the spirit of wider questioning. What to eat? What to wear? What to do now? How to make ends meet and negotiate life's trials with scarce resources? Or how to console oneself for life's failures by grasping after the hollow happiness that a seemingly endless array of consumable goods holds out to one? We are too busy grasping at life or fending off its assaults for anything more; wrung out by the day to day, our need for meaning is silenced, put to sleep.

This silencing of the question of meaning in everyday life is reinforced by the predominance of other sorts of *why* questions in the modern West. The shift to a scientific mentality in the early modern period was bound up with the emergence of efficient causality as a sufficient explanation for happenings within the world. Explaining something meant showing how it came to be in terms of prior causes acting without intelligence or design. Asking why we are here becomes, on those terms, equivalent to the question of how human beings came to be on the planet. It is, in that case, a question to be answered in the familiar terms of evolutionary theory, in terms of chemical and biological processes that start with the conditions favoring life on this planet and end with the requisite random mutations to the DNA of our apelike ancestors.

Why are we here? as a question about the meaning of life is not the question the scientist is answering in terms of efficient causality, but the two sorts of questions are easily conflated in modern times. How the two come to be confused is illuminated by the account the famous anthropologist Mary Douglas liked to give of common errors in Western interpretations of African witchcraft beliefs. The Azande invoke witchcraft when, say, a granary falls on a man, killing him instantly. Western anthropologists commonly presumed that such accusations of witchcraft meant the Azande lacked any conception of a scientific account of causal links within the natural world. The Western observer knows that a granary falls because of feeble support structures and a strong wind — witchcraft has nothing to do with it. The Azande, however, as Douglas points out, are asking a different sort of question, a question about meaning: Why did this granary fall just now, killing just this man and no one else? The Azande are not asking a question about efficient causality — about causes that they, like their Western counterparts, know quite well — they are asking a "why me?" question, one that Westerners might answer in terms of bad luck or the will of God.

Whatever one might think of witchcraft as an answer to this "why me?" question, the Western failure to understand the distinctive character of the question reveals something about broad cultural trends in the West during the period of colonial expansion. The same confusion of different types of questions that one finds in this uncharitable interpretation of non-Western cultural practices lurks behind the subordination of religion to science in evolutionary accounts of culture familiar in the West since the nineteenth century. The cultural force of religion is to be replaced by science in modern times — the natural and social sciences make religion obsolete — because science offers a better explanation for why things are the way they are. By putting religion and science on a single line of cultural progress in this fashion, one mistakenly presumes that religious people are asking the sort of questions that modern science answers. Any question of meaning beyond the range of scientific explanation is thereby eclipsed.

If then we assume to the contrary that Why are we here? is a distinctive sort of question, one that religion rather than science has the better resources for tackling, what kind of answer might Christianity give to it? Most generally, when offering a response, Christians talk about the purposes and intentions that God has with respect to human beings. God creates the world with certain ends in mind for human beings (indeed, for the rest of the beings that comprise the world). The frustration or modes of achievement of those ends make up the traditional topics of theological discussion. Thus, *sin* means the frustration of God's intentions or purposes by the errant exercise of human free will. *Providence* concerns God's plans in their implementation throughout the general course of human history. *Incarnation* is the primary means and defining moment of God's intentions with respect to the world. *Salvation* is a way of talking about the effects on human life should God's intentions be realized. *The end of the world* — the final things that theologians discuss under the rubric of *eschatology* — is God's intentions come to final fruition. In short, Christians answer the question, Why are we here? by looking at what God wants for us; God's expectations for us set the frame within which human life is given its meaning.

Christian theologians characterize God's purposes and intentions for us in a variety of ways. On one view, we are here to be raised up by degrees beyond ourselves into the divine life; being made like God, we are to be in communion with God, or despite the continuing differences between us, we are to enjoy God's presence. On another view, we are here exactly as we are to live as the friends or children of God, or perhaps to be God's partners in history, furthering God's own liberation projects. On still other views, we are here to glorify and magnify God, a goodness and a greatness that are not ours, through our praise and worship. Or we are here to manifest in our being and actions the goodness of God graciously communicated to us, imitating God's holiness as best we are able, living lives of perfect obedience to God's will.

Whatever their disagreements on particulars or differences in emphasis, all these characterizations of God's purposes and intentions suggest, at the most general level of description, that we are here to be in relation to God. We are to be with God; that is why we are here. Our lives have meaning in virtue of a relationship with God, a relationship that comes to expression in all the variety of forms just mentioned. In a way, there is nothing exceptional about living one's life in a relationship with God. All creatures do this, willy-nilly, whether they like it not. Creatures just *are* in a relationship with God. Christian beliefs about creation affirm this at a very fundamental level. Everything that exists gets its existence from God. Without a relationship like that to God, there would simply be nothing. One could say, then, that human beings along with the rest of God's creatures are not simply *in* a relationship with God; they *are* that relationship in the sense that such a relationship constitutes their very being.

It follows that a continuing relationship with God is the condition of our continuing to live, move, and breathe. Despite our efforts to break off relations with God — a turning away from God in disbelief, anger, or distraction, which manifests itself in the disordered use of our capacities — God must, it appears, be maintaining, from God's side, a relationship with us. The world is under God's constant purview, one might say; the world forms the ever-present object of divine concern. This is what Christian beliefs about God's providence and God's initiatives as Redeemer affirm quite strongly. Nothing can separate us from God. The Christian insistence on God's graciousness, a graciousness exhibited definitively for Christians in God's workings in Jesus Christ, extends in this way a central motif of the Hebrew Bible — the motif of God's steadfast love and faithfulness.

If all creatures are in a relationship with God, not all of them are aware of that fact, not all of them have the freedom, consequently, to choose, with full consciousness, whether to align themselves with that fact or not. This is the special prerogative of human beings; this is why *human beings* are here.

In virtue of capacities that set them off from the rest of creation, human beings may become conscious of the relationship that they, and the whole of creation, enjoy with God. Orienting their lives around such an awareness, their affections, cognitive faculties, volitions, and deeds should become a register of that relationship. Gratitude and praise for God's gifts, an other-directed love without anxious self-concern and an unshakable sense of one's worth in God's sight, a joyful peace and simple trust in God, should all well up in response. One's mind should rejoice in the careful tracings of God's presence and influence. God's purposes should become the spontaneous desires of one's own heart and be matched by one's utmost efforts to see them realized.

When human beings direct their lives properly in this way according to their own free decisions and inclinations — when, that is, they choose the character of their lives so as to show a proper respect for the relationship that creatures enjoy with God — the dumb mirror of God that is the world has added to it an eloquent witness. This, Christian theologians often suggest, is what it means to say that human beings are created in the image of God. It is their prerogative among the myriad creatures of God to reflect self-consciously the relationship with God that the world as a whole shows forth in its very being.

This very basic Christian answer to the question, Why are we here? provides then a life-orienting framework of meaning within which one can place the details of one's everyday existence. It is a meaning-giving framework sufficiently elastic to suffuse the whole of the day-to-day and every stage of life's way. In every affair of life — in public or private, in word or deed, when active or in retirement, in matters of state or worries about economic justice, when contemplating the course of either the natural world or human history, when assessing the character of one's desires or deciding one's responsibilities to one's neighbors, when helping others or caring for oneself — one can try to witness self-consciously, in one's feelings, thoughts, and deeds, to the relationship that creatures enjoy with God. In short, one tries self-consciously to inscribe the relationship one has with God everywhere. By shaping one's existence in accordance with the recognition of a relationship enjoyed with God, one comes, in effect, to worship God in and through the character of one's whole life.

If the point of human life is to be in relation to God, one's life is made meaningful by being set within the widest possible framework of significance. It is true that in virtue of this Christian orientation one's life is given a meaning in and for itself. Despite the strong corporate sense here of a responsibility that human beings share, Christianity holds firm to the idea that God has a relationship with each one of us, demonstrating a special concern on God's part for every individual as such. One is charged, then, with being an eloquent witness to the relationship creatures enjoy with God in a way that distinctly exhibits one's own special talents and character. But one is nevertheless carried beyond oneself here, beyond even the context of human concern, according to a meaning-giving vision of world-encompassing scope. Whatever the special duties that accrue to the human species or to particular human persons in virtue of their unique capacities, one's own life is given meaning only insofar as it is brought under the umbrella of a relationship with God enjoyed by the whole world as the creation of God and the object of God's continuing concern.

This meaning to life is also lasting. Its pertinence is not threatened by disappointment and loss. Should one find the point to one's life in raising good children or writing good books or furthering the liberation of humankind or convincing others of the beauty and goodness of God's creation, meaning is lost when one's hopes for these activities are. Living a life that recognizes the relationship that one enjoys with God does, indeed, fund or promote enterprises of these sorts; such enterprises are appropriate responses to a sense of one's relationship with God. But one's relationship with God remains available as an orienting focus for life despite their failure.

We are called to reflect in thought, word, and deed our relationship with God, but such enterprises are not what calls that relationship into being or what keeps it afloat. Established and maintained by a God who keeps faith with us, that relationship is therefore not jeopardized by the fragility or corruption of human performance in response to it. Christians are convinced one simply has this relationship in virtue of the graciousness of God displayed in Christ no matter how inhospitable the circumstances or serious one's personal shortcomings. One's relation to a God of steadfast love and faithfulness continues to beckon, therefore, as a point of reference for a redirected human life regardless of how difficult are the personal or structural obstacles to a life that reflects that relation effectively. Indeed, this persistent meaning-giving, life-directing capacity of a relationship with God is the import of the cross and resurrection: God remains with us, and God remains our God, despite the disappointment of what God rightly expects from us, despite sin and death and the apparent end of all hope for God's kingdom in this-worldly terms.

By complicating the significance of successful performance in this way, the Christian answer to the question, Why are we here? subverts an especially common way of addressing the question of meaning in the modern West, where the meaning of human lives is often assessed in terms of their functions, in terms of the tasks or jobs they perform. In short, they are assessed with reference to their productivity in a means-to-ends calculation. Although something of this sort has always been a possibility, in contemporary times the means-to-ends calculations appropriate to the running of an efficient bureaucracy or a profitable business venture infiltrate as never before people's sense of the point of their lives. The result is a kind of overidentification with role performance so that the tasks with which I identify — performing my job, raising my children — take with them all sense of a meaningful life when they go. What is an old woman worth, without husband or family to attend to? What is an unemployed life worth, one that makes no economic contribution to the wealth of the nation?

Questions like these are not just broached by unsympathetic outsiders but by the individuals at issue themselves. What I do — and doing it well — is my reason for being. Apart from the performance of such tasks, there is little point to carrying on.

Finding the meaning of human life in the purposes or intentions of God might suggest a similar stress on the proper performance of tasks: human life has meaning to the extent human beings carry out those divine purposes or intentions. God does not just have expectations for us in that case. God has a wider agenda that we are to serve. God's expectations for us involve us as a means to some further end. Answering the question, Why are we here? by talking about what God wants from us would mean, then, thinking of our relationship with God in terms of being hired to perform a job. Looking around the world, contemplating the circumstances of our lives, and asking of the God who presumably brought us here for some reason, "Why are we here?" would be something like wandering around a job site, ignorant of the intentions of one's would-be employer, and asking, "What are the tasks that our boss in bringing us here has in mind for us to perform?" The *why* in the question anticipates an answer in terms of a means/ends relationship; it points to a response in terms of some set of ends for which we are to supply the means.

While the Christian answer to the question of meaning does stress, as we have seen, the importance of human activity, in some fundamental way it undercuts the sense that human beings are here to serve God's purposes. Christian theologians are making a point like this when they affirm that God's purposes and intentions with respect to the world are not based on need. Human beings are not useful to God. God does not need human beings to perform any sort of task; God's relations with human beings do not suppose that God needs something to be done, something that human beings are to do their part to bring about. God does not even need human beings for company. It is not simply the case that God does not need human beings to do something; God does not need human beings at all. The existence of human beings, Christian theologians commonly say, satisfies no demand of God's nature. God does not have to create the world. Instead, human beings are here, they enjoy a relationship with God, because of a purely gratuitous act of beneficence on God's part.

If human beings are to respond properly to such a gratuitous act of generosity and love on God's part, certain forms of action are appropriate. That God does not need human beings is therefore not an excuse to renege on our responsibilities to live in ways appropriate to that relationship. We are required, say, to mirror the character of God's relations with us by demonstrating a similar gift-giving and upbuilding relationship with our fellow creatures. We are, nevertheless, not here as a requirement for the achievement of a community like that. We are obligated to work for communities of justice and peace; these are the sort of communities that should result from our efforts to shape our lives self-consciously in conformity with our relationship to God. But, at a more fundamental level, the reason we are here has nothing to do with being a means to such an end. This is so because, one might say, what God expects *for* us is not simply equivalent to what God expects *of* us. That God has expectations for us does indeed entail that God has expectations of us — we are required to act accordingly. But our efforts are not the measure of what God can bring about for us; what God wants for us can exceed what God expects of us. Thus, Christians commonly believe that God's expectations for us include a personal and social good that exceeds any human capacity to carry out.

The fact that God does not enter into relation with us to serve a purpose is, furthermore, made incontrovertibly clear by God's relations with things that seemingly have no purpose. As the magnificent speeches of God from out of the whirlwind in the Book of Job suggest quite strongly, God shows a provi-

dential concern even for beings that serve no ends to which
human beings can ascribe any significance — beings, such as
mountain goats and wild donkeys, that are of no use to human
existence; creatures so irregular and exceptional (e.g., Behe-
moth and Leviathan) that they mock the ordinary run of human
life; beings whose activities seem singularly unproductive even
within their own sphere. So, the ostrich, without the least sign
of a prudential intelligence, "leaves her eggs on the ground with
only earth to warm them; forgetting that a foot may tread on
them or a wild animal crush them. Cruel to her chicks as if
they were not hers, little she cares if her labour goes for nothing" (Job 39:13–18). God's plan, God's intentions and purposes
for the world, include events that go to waste, like rain on barren ground, and efforts of expenditure without return — "their
calves, having grown big and strong, go off into the desert and
never come back to them" (39:4). What are we to say, then, of
human lives that also come to nothing?

God's speeches to Job, which conform so well to a Christian stress on the gratuity of God's relations to the world, show
how God delights even in what is useless and worthless by
human estimation, even in what is unproductive according to
any means-to-ends calculation that human beings can understand. The "meaning" of human life is thereby fundamentally
redefined, set upon a new basis. We are certainly called by God
to be productive — to use our gifts for ends that conform with
our understanding of how to live in response to God — but
the Christian answer to the question, Why are we here? suggests that the meaning of our lives exceeds anything that can
be discussed in those terms. God is the God, too, of times that
are barren and of spheres of existence that seem to open out
onto a desolate, fruitless waste. God accompanies us even then,
even there.

For Further Reading

Because of the breadth of the topic, almost any work in Christian theology
is germane, but listed below are some that might especially spur further
reflection on how to assess the worth of human life.

Augustine. *Confessions.* Translated with an introduction by John K. Ryan. New York: Doubleday, 1960. The premier retrospective reflection on the course of one's life by one of Christianity's most influential theologians.

Kierkegaard, Søren. *Training in Christianity.* Translated with an introduction by Walter Lowrie. Princeton: Princeton University Press, 1967. Kierkegaard with his usual wit and incisiveness comments on the shape of human living that makes Jesus Christ its paradigm.

Pascal, Blaise. *Pensées.* Translated with an introduction by A. J. Krailsheimer. London: Penguin, 1966. A seventeenth-century member of a persecuted Catholic minority discusses the meaning of life in the face of relativism, moral laxness, and the search for cheap amusements.

Schleiermacher, Friedrich. *On Religion: Speeches to Its Cultured Despisers.* Translated with an introduction by Richard Crouten. Cambridge: Cambridge University Press, 1988. A famous Protestant theologian of the nineteenth century explores how to live religiously in the modern world.

2

WHY ARE WE SO INDIFFERENT ABOUT OUR SPIRITUAL LIVES?

David Dawson

I am sometimes shaken out of my indifference by a memory. It usually begins with the weather that day, ten years ago: a brilliant, cold early December morning, the low sunlight forcing me to squint as I say good-bye to my wife in front of the terminal, the crisp air briefly filling my lungs with that satisfying burn that mountain climbers will recognize. Then I am in the warm interior of the cabin; I and the others lean back in our seats as the Boeing 737 ascends steeply, twin jet engines at full throttle. The memory fast forwards again, and we are eight minutes into our climb. There is the first loud thump on the right side of the plane, and the aircraft shudders. Turbulence, I think — but what is that strange metallic sound? Several minutes drag by; there is murmuring among the passengers on the right side of the plane, then the second, louder, more angry thump, and the aircraft lurches. A middle-aged man sitting across the aisle announces softly, in an oddly matter-of-fact voice, "Well, it's gone now." "What do you mean?" I ask. "The right engine has fallen off the wing. It was hanging for a minute or two, but now it's gone." Time begins to crawl; the cabin attendants seem to move in slow motion as a series of buzzers go off, but my mind is racing: Did the engine take anything else with it? Control cables? Fuel lines? No one knows. The plane is now swaying, descending in a slow, rocking turn. The cabin speaker crackles: "Ladies and gentlemen, as you are aware, we have a problem. We are returning to Philly. Our hands will be full from this point on; please follow the directions of the flight attendants." My throat

17

tightens a few more notches when one of those flight attendants tells us to stuff eyeglasses, pens, and other sharp objects into our socks. I comply, and my last illusion of control vanishes as the faces around me dissolve into a nearsighted blur. I had watched the tanker truck beside us before takeoff; I suspect we have a full load of fuel. During the next ten minutes, I try to get ready for what will happen.

How did I get ready? Did I, confessing my sins, "make my peace with God"? Did I mount a silent Job-like protest to God? Did I offer up a request for some timely divine intervention? Such questions are familiar to us; submission to God's will, protest against God's will, and pleas for God's intervention may come close to exhausting what most of us think of whenever moments of distress prompt us to consider our "spiritual lives." But I did none of these things (I must even admit that the thought of God did not occur to me). Instead, my mind's eye flashed back and forth between two possible endings for this chapter in the story of my life. First, the good ending, for one of the early chapters: the engine has dropped cleanly; the pilot is adept at single-engine landings; we land safely; and my wife, parents, friends, and colleagues rejoice at my survival. Then, the bad ending of what turns out to be the final chapter: the falling engine has taken other vital airplane parts with it; the pilot's training makes no difference; we explode in a fireball on impact; and my wife, parents, friends, and colleagues grieve at my death. My mind soon discards its Hollywood images of the landing or the crash, settling instead on the postcrash reactions of persons to whom I was (had been?) closely related.

It has often been observed that because we cannot imagine what we have never experienced, we cannot imagine our own deaths. Instead, we imagine the reactions to our deaths of those with whom we have significant relationships. Later that afternoon, on the long Amtrak run to Boston (I had lost my enthusiasm for flying any more that day), my reflections took a curious turn: my imagination of others' grief at my death slowly changed into an image of my grief for them, as though we had exchanged places, and they had been the ones on a doomed flight. Writing this essay has made me wonder again about these two strangely related responses to the possibility of my own death. Granted that we think the unthinkable thought of our own deaths by imagining the reactions of loved ones to it, but why did my imagination of others' grief over my death so readily become an imagination of my grief over theirs? Considering this question rather than more obviously "spiritual" questions about accepting or resisting God's will, or pleading for God's aid, can bring us to deeper recognition of our spiritual life, as well as to the forms of our indifference about it.

Our Loneliness

In promising to cut us off from everything, death — or rather, the prospect of our own deaths — threatens us with complete isolation. Though we hide from this threat, it is always there, made nearly palpable to us in periods of genuine loneliness, barely intimated in those brief, passing put-downs, snubs, curt replies, and acts of inattention that pervade our daily lives, reminding us of just how easily we can be cut off from others. Yet if the prospect of our deaths should ever become real for us — if only for ten minutes — it can make nearly intolerable our suspicion that, at the end of the day, when all the rites have been completed and all the candles have burned out, we will be left utterly alone, without a single companion. In rare moments, when something as unpredictable as metal fatigue catches us off guard and the engine falls, we might glimpse our radical loneliness, but even then we are likely to replace that vision with excessive, self-assuring images of the deep-felt love others have for us. Most of the time, though, the metal holds, the hours imperceptibly slip by, and we bury our occasional intimations of mortality under what Wordsworth called "the lethargy of custom," that vast collection of illusions and diversions we refer to as our lives.

I sense the need for some definitions at this point, so I turn to a nearby dictionary:

> *life:* "the quality that distinguishes a vital and functional being from a dead body"

> *death:* "a permanent cessation of all vital functions: the end of life"

These definitions reflect our ordinary usage exactly: we define life and death in direct opposition to each other, but we do not let them characterize the same space of time. Instead, we imagine a sequence: first there is nothing; then comes our life; and then that life comes to a permanent end, which we call *death*. Life is the absence of death; then comes death, which is the absence of life. Saint Augustine also saw life and death as opposites, but he discerned in their mutual exclusivity an implication more radical than any ventured by *Webster's Ninth New Collegiate Dictionary*. Augustine observed that what we call *life* is, in reality, a single, extended act of dying. Each passing second is the passing away of life; from the moment of our birth, the end is already upon us, and we pass each subsequent day by literally passing away.

Where, then, *is* our life? Wherever it is, it is clearly not in our hands — it is not *with* us at all. But if this is the truth about our so-called lives, it is a truth too great for us to bear: we do everything in our power to avoid it. We begin with calendars and clocks, by which we try to block time's flow by carving it up into discrete "time blocks." We then fill up the blocks or blanks of time with our activities, which serve to give us something to think about besides the flow of time, the inexorable ebbing away that is our lives. Above all, though we say we yearn for more free time, we avoid it like the plague, preferring instead to seek out periods of leisure time, during which we pursue leisure activities. And if we are successful, if we can keep the calendar full and time moving under our control, we can continue to live as though we believed our greatest illusion — that we are immortal.

This week my family is preparing for our first serious leisure-time activity of the summer. We are going tent camping for the first time ever, planning for which now threatens to rival the complexity of a space-shuttle launch. My wife and I had not mentioned a single word to our children about bears (there are in fact black bears where we are headed), but yesterday my six-year-old son Aaron asked pointedly, "What if there are bears at the campsite?" Caught a bit off guard (as I have been for six years now), I dodged Socratically: "Well, what do you think you would do if you saw a bear?" He answered without hesitation and with noticeable certitude: "I would turn around and run for my life." Silly boy. Like Simmias in Plato's *Phaedo*, my son clearly stands in need of an introduction to philosophy (or rather, as a former philosopher colleague of mine used to call it, in hushed tones, Philosophy). Had I been quick enough on my feet not only to talk like Socrates but to think like him, I might have led my son at once down the following well-worn path:

Me: Son, is not what we call death a freeing and separation of soul from body?

Him: Sure, Dad [six-year-olds will still, on occasion, naively grant a fatal opening premise].

Me: And the desire to free the soul is found chiefly, or rather only, in the true philosopher. In fact the philosopher's occupation consists precisely in the freeing and separation of soul from body. Isn't that so?

Him: It seems so, Dad.

Me: Well then, as I said at the beginning, if a man has trained himself throughout his life to live in a state as close as possible to death, would it not be ridiculous for him to be distressed when death comes to him?

Him: It sure would, Dad. Of course.

Me: Then it is a fact, Aaron, that true philosophers make dying their profession and that to them, of all men, death is least alarming. Look at it in this way. If they are thoroughly dissatisfied with the body and long to have their souls independent of it, when this happens, would it not be entirely unreasonable to be frightened and distressed? Would they not naturally be glad to set out for the place where there is a prospect of attaining the object of their lifelong desire — which is wisdom — and of escaping from an unwelcome association? Surely there are many who have chosen of their own free will to follow dead lovers and wives and sons to the next world, in the hope of seeing and meeting there the persons whom they loved. If this is so, will a true lover of wisdom who has firmly grasped this same conviction — that he will never attain to wisdom worthy of the name elsewhere than in the next world — will he be grieved at dying? Will he not be glad to make that journey? We must suppose so, my dear boy, that is, if he is a real philosopher, because then he will be of the firm belief that he will never find wisdom in all its purity in any other place. If this is so, would it not be

quite unreasonable, as I said just now, for such a man to be afraid
of death?

Him: It would, indeed. OK, I'm ready. Let's go camping!

(Plato, *Phaedo* 67D–68B, slightly modified)

We might find a certain mordant humor in this interchange if
we did not recognize it as disturbingly representative of much
mainstream Western intellectual and popular thought about life
and death. Like the members of the now notorious Heaven's
Gate and (I would wager) a sizable portion of the membership of mainstream Christian churches, Socrates believed that
human personhood resides in an immortal soul whose fullest
life is impeded by the presence of a body (I must note that
such a view is decidedly non-Christian, for Christians affirm
the resurrection of the body rather than the immortality of the
soul as one's entry into full human personhood). Socrates' perspective can easily lead us to a certain insouciance in the face
of death ("would it not be ridiculous...to be distressed when
death comes?") and, correspondingly, to a certain satisfaction
with our own inalienable immortality.

Do we really live under the illusion that we are immortal?
How could this be when we are surrounded by a veritable
culture of death — from indiscriminate drive-by shootings, to
murderous acts of domestic terrorism, to daily child and spouse
abuse behind closed doors? Nonetheless, the mere existence
of reality does nothing to discourage a truly serviceable self-
deception; we persist in living the illusion of immortality as
though it were our reality. We live it as we utter caustic remarks
to loved ones in the implicit certitude that we and they will be
present tomorrow to start again with a clean slate; we live it
as we see and do not perceive the graying hairs, the slowing
gait, the disenchantments of aging parents; we live it even as
we imagine ourselves still alive after our deaths, reassured re-
cipients of the grief of our loved ones, who, unlike ourselves,
are momentarily under the illusion that we have really died.
And yet, like the tremor of mortality it suppresses, confidence
in our own immortality is strongest when least examined, when
hidden from sight, where it can operate unimpeded as the un-
questioned premise, the unexamined given. For the more our

assumption of immortality is made explicit, the less believable it becomes, even to us lesser deities.

Our Diversions

We are unwilling to bring either awareness of mortality or illusion of immortality to the surface of our explicit attention. The more we recognize our mortality, the more exposed our pretense of immortality appears to us, thereby failing to perform its useful magic. Where will we find our smoke and mirrors? How will we keep ourselves from looking up our own sleeves? The only thing to do is to find something *to do*. For if we have nothing to do, we will be faced directly with ourselves — and that, writes the seventeenth-century Augustinian Blaise Pascal in his *Pensées*, is something we will avoid at all costs. Instead of examining ourselves, we will always find something else to care about:

> From childhood on...[persons] are made responsible for the care of their honour, their property, their friends, and even of the property and honour of their friends; they are burdened with duties, language-training and exercises, and given to understand that they can never be happy unless their health, their honour, their fortune and those of their friends are in good shape, and that it needs only one thing to go wrong to make them unhappy. So they are given responsibilities and duties which harass them from the first moment of each day. You will say that is an odd way to make them happy: what better means could one devise to make them unhappy? What could one do? You would only have to take away all their cares, and then they would see themselves and think about what they are, where they come from, and where they are going.

To be indifferent is to be care-less, without care. But to say that we are indifferent about our spiritual lives is to recognize that our indifference about life is a willed indifference about who we really are: it is to be *without care* for ourselves *as a form of desire*. To be spiritually indifferent is *not to care* one way or another about our own lives, but instead *to care* about everything else. We turn outward to the things around us and away from ourselves as we are; paradoxically, we become care-less by multiplying our cares (I originally typed in the phrase

"multiplying our cars," which, for the upper-middle-class sub-
urb I live in, may drive the point home especially well). Pascal
says that we are in fact utterly consumed with cares, by which
we divert ourselves from serious introspection; we fill our time
with cares "so that there should never be an empty moment"
to look into ourselves, for "the natural unhappiness of our feeble mortal condition" is "so wretched that nothing can console
us when we really think about it." "The only good thing,"
concludes Pascal, is for people "to be diverted from thinking
of what they are, either by some occupation which takes their
mind off it, or by some novel and agreeable passion which keeps
them busy, like gambling, hunting, some absorbing show, in
short by what is called diversion." "That is why men are so
fond of hustle and bustle; that is why prison is such a fearful
punishment; that is why the pleasures of solitude are so incomprehensible." To protect our illusion of immortality, we must
keep ourselves from any intimation of our mortality — and that
requires us always to be busy thinking about something else:
"Being unable to cure death, wretchedness and ignorance, men
have decided, in order to be happy, not to think about such
things."

Near catastrophes that catch us off guard may sometimes
force us to confront truths about ourselves that we would otherwise choose not to face. But do they tell us anything about us
that we could not learn through other, more subtle forms of attention? Might they not simply illumine, for a moment, deep
and pervasive truths about our lives that we easily overlook
or find convenient to ignore? We do not need to find ourselves
aboard a crippled airliner to be confronted by our loneliness or
comforted by our diversions. All of this can happen in the pri-
vacy of our own rooms. Let us sit alone with ourselves. Let's
just try it. Before three minutes have passed, most of us will
be uncomfortable. At ten minutes, the boredom will have become suffocating, and we will start to fret about wasting time.
Well before the fifteen-minute mark, we will have already found
an agreeable diversion — the fly over there on the chair, that
pattern in the wallpaper. Before the twenty-minute mark ar-
rives, we will be off to the store for groceries, on the phone to
a friend, or surfing the web. We late-twentieth-century people

just cannot stand to be bored, and when we are left alone with ourselves, with "nothing but time on our hands," we rapidly become bored — and soon, instead of just "marking time" or "wasting" it," we "fill it," putting it to "good use." (Just a few Sundays ago I was surprised to hear a minister declare in his sermon that those of us who evade our responsibilities with the excuse "I don't have enough time" are never without time "to do something for God." But why am I surprised? The gospel of grace is so often replaced with the gospel of trying harder, which, after all, is something we can, after rolling up our sleeves, get to work on.)

Every so often, despite ourselves, we may recognize that boredom is the presence of death in the midst of our lives. The adolescent mantra "BOR-ing," now become our favored catchall complaint, is how life as the process of dying *feels* to us in the midst of our ordinary, everyday lives. And yet, though we instinctively locate boredom outside us (those people are so boring; that film was so boring; my job is so boring), we also sometimes recognize that we are personally implicated in our own boredom.

Boredom is an indifference about our lives that combines desire with the negation of desire, with paralysis as the consequence. Such indifference is not totally dismissive, altogether without care (for why would I bother to write an essay about *that*, and why would you bother to read it? When they are not diversions, writing and reading can be acts of protest against such sweeping indifference, such all-pervasive boredom). No, this indifference is a willful short circuit, a desired failure of follow-through: I may sometimes sense a profound need to live a more spiritual life, but nonetheless I simply do not do it. It is not that I try to live such a life and fail at it; rather, at the very outset of my desire to live such a life, indeed present in that very desire, is my desire not to. Such indifference takes us beyond the orbit of contemporary discussions of boredom such as that offered recently by literary historian and critic Patricia Meyer Spacks, who analyzes contemporary boredom as a bland apathy characterized by the assumption of entitlement without any corresponding sense of responsibility (the world exists to amuse me; I deserve to be entertained). In contrast, the indif-

ference I am probing here cannot escape the realm of personal
responsibility, for it is not simply the absence of desire; it is a
perverse desire against desire.

In his *Pensées*, Pascal described this conflict between desires
at the center of the state he called *ennui*. Aristocrats seeking
to escape ennui through diversion are torn between two dimensions of their creatureliness. On the one hand, they "have
a secret instinct driving them to seek external diversion and
occupation, and this is the result of their constant sense of
wretchedness." But on the other hand, "they have another secret instinct, left over from the greatness of our original nature,
telling them that the only true happiness lies in rest and not in
excitement." These "two contrary instincts give rise to a confused plan buried out of sight in the depths of their soul, which
leads them to seek rest by way of activity and always to imagine that the satisfaction they miss will come to them once they
overcome certain obvious difficulties and can open the door
to welcome rest." Pascal sums up the aristocrat's state as our
own: "All our life passes in this way: we seek rest by struggling against certain obstacles, and once they are overcome, rest
proves intolerable because of the boredom [*ennui*] it produces.
We must get away from it and crave excitement."

We get hints of this inner dynamic when we return from our
carefully planned, ambitious vacations, and virtually upon our
return (if not during the trip back home), we encounter the
void — our own void — again. In his essay "Self-Reliance,"
Emerson scorned such travel: he knew that either we travel in
order to leave part of ourselves behind (a futile act since we invariably bring all of ourselves along for the ride), or we travel
in order to find ourselves (a redundant act since we are always
already alone with ourselves at home):

> Traveling is a fool's paradise. Our first journeys discover to us the
> indifference of places. At home I dream that at Naples, at Rome,
> I can be intoxicated with beauty, and lose my sadness. I pack my
> trunk, embrace my friends, embark on the sea, and at last wake
> up in Naples, and there beside me is the stern fact, the sad self,
> unrelenting, identical, that I fled from. I seek the Vatican, and the
> palaces. I affect to be intoxicated with sights and suggestions, but I
> am not intoxicated. My giant goes with me wherever I go.

Emerson regards travel much the way Pascal assesses the aristo-crat's hunting or gaming — as a diversion, a delaying tactic, the forestalling of a question.

Pascal's analysis of ennui challenges our typically constricted sense of what might count as the "spiritual" dimension of our lives: spiritual life is not some special portion or subset of life; it is simply life as such, life as it really is, in contrast to self-deceptive, self-serving diversions. And spiritual life is not some sort of escape from the constraints of ordinary, embodied, phys-ical life; the opposite of the word *spiritual* is not *material* but *illusory*. To recognize our lives as already spiritual is to rec-ognize two contrary truths about the only life we live: we are mortal, fallen beings, yet we are promised (by virtue of our cre-ation "according to the image" of an immortal, infinite Deity) an immortal destiny; there is a divinely intended trajectory to human existence (rest) that has been provisionally undermined by human sinfulness (wretchedness).

Pascal's reflections echo the famous opening lines of Augus-tine's *Confessions*:

> You are great, Lord, and highly to be praised: great is your power and your wisdom is immeasurable. *Humanity, a little piece of your creation, desires to praise you*, a human being bearing his mor-tality with him, carrying with him the witness of his sin and the witness that you resist the proud. Nevertheless, *to praise you is the desire of humanity, a little piece of your creation.* You stir human beings to take pleasure in praising you, because you have made us for yourself, and our heart is restless until it rests in you. (emphasis added)

Augustine carefully positions his remark about human fallen-ness between reiterations of the human desire to praise God, highlighting the priority of that instinct "left over from the greatness of our original nature." While Augustine in this pas-sage emphasizes our instinct for God, Pascal focuses on our instinct for diversion — the sense of wretchedness that is the felt consequence of the death that Augustine calls the witness of sin and sin's punishment. Pascal here draws on a distinction Augustine liked to make between mortality and death. Augus-tine argued that while human beings are properly *mortal* by virtue of being finite creatures, God never intended for mortal human beings *to die*. Mortality was a condition for the possibility of death, but the actual death of human beings was a contingent event that served as the penalty for human sin. When Pascal speaks of the "sense of wretchedness" then, he refers to a person's anxious awareness of his or her impending death as a penalty for sin. Pascal focuses on isolation as the heart of this sense of wretchedness, the isolation feared, for example, by the king who refuses to "stay quietly in his room." Such kings are "surrounded by people who are incredibly careful to see that the king should never be alone and able to think about himself." For to be alone is to risk thinking about oneself; to think about oneself is to face one's impending death; and death threatens one with final isolation. Pascal understood that we do not fear dying so much as we fear dying alone; he would understand well just why even the thought of spending our final days in a nursing home can make our skin crawl. We will do whatever it takes to eliminate the specter of final isolation:

> That is why this man, who lost his only son a few months ago...is not thinking about it anymore. Do not be surprised; he is concentrating all his attention on which way the boar will go that his dogs have been so hotly pursuing for the past six hours. That is all he needs. However sad a man may be, if you can persuade him to take up some diversion he will be happy while it lasts, and however happy a man may be, if he lacks diversion and has no absorbing passion or entertainment to keep boredom away, he will soon be depressed and unhappy. Without diversion there is no joy; with diversion there is no sadness.

Our Spiritual Good

"Without diversion there is no joy; with diversion there is no sadness." Pascal's aphorism is ironic, of course, for his own analysis suggests that diversion can lead to no true or lasting joy and that the state from which one seeks to be diverted is the very essence of sadness. Pascal's language may strike many of us as odd. How often do we think of our boredom as a matter of sorrow? How often do we think of boredom's antithesis — interest or desire — as a matter of joy? We are readily bored, perhaps less readily interested, only occasionally thrilled or excited — but how often are we sad or joyous? Our contemporary language of boredom and interest seems thin and flat by comparison with richer, more profound words like *sadness* and *joy*, or with the biblical language of *blessedness* or *beatitude*. Yet to understand boredom as the penumbra of sorrow, or interest as the intimation of joy, is to see more deeply into the character of the human condition, as it is with God and as it is in flight from God.

In order to grasp our "champing wish, stalled with our lassitude" as a matter of our relation to God, it helps to move backwards in time, from accounts of contemporary boredom as apathetic entitlement without responsibility, through early modern Pascalian reflections on the contrary desires of a sinful creature created in the divine image, to earlier accounts of that perplexing condition ancient and medieval Christians called *acedia* or "spiritual indifference." *Acedia* is derived from the Greek *akēdeia* or *a-kēdos*, "without care." In the third and fourth centuries, hermits and monks such as John Cassian spoke of "the noontide demon," the disturbing combination of indifference, lassitude, and restlessness about one's spiritual discipline that frequently overcame desert ascetics in the heat of the day. Saint Thomas Aquinas wrote about it in the thirteenth century, at the culmination of many centuries of diverse Christian reflections on the experience of listlessness, despondency, or sloth in living the ascetic or monastic life. Thomas makes two points about spiritual indifference that Pascal does not emphasize: spiritual indifference is first of all a sin — a willful act of opposition to God. And this act of opposition to God is fundamentally an opposition to love — to God's love for us and in us, and to God's invitation to us to extend love to others.

In his *Summa Theologiae*, Thomas defines the sin of acedia as "sorrow over spiritual good." Acedia is not a sin because it is an emotion, for emotions in themselves are not sins; we are perfectly justified in sorrowing over evil, but we should not sorrow over what is good. Acedia is blameworthy because it is radically *misplaced* sorrow, sorrow directed against our own spiritual good. What is our spiritual good? For Thomas, it is the goodness of God's love for us, as it is received by us. The person beset by acedia is sorrowful over the divine good, not as a good located somewhere outside the self, but precisely insofar as he or she can and does already participate in it. The spiritually indifferent person sorrows over the divine good as his or her own God-given orientation toward his or her proper spiritual destiny. Spiritual apathy, therefore, is not simply "mentally running from any spiritual good you can think of, but from the divine good to which we should cleave" — it is running away from the God who is already present to oneself. There is, then, in Thomas's eyes something willfully perverse about the state of acedia: one does not *suffer* from it; one *commits* it. One commits a kind of spiritual suicide, willfully cutting oneself off from one's life in God. That is why Thomas writes that "spiritual apathy goes against the command to keep the Sabbath holy. In so far as that is a moral command, it tells us to let our minds rest in God." But as Pascal observed, we look outside of ourselves (but not to God) in order to secure that rest. Or as Thomas put it, acedia "seeks wrongful relaxation in so far as it spurns good." The spurious rest that follows dissolves at once into restlessness.

Just as Thomas, unlike Pascal, highlights the willful opposition that characterizes indifference, so too he, unlike Pascal, identifies love as the target of the indifferent person's opposition. To be sorrowful about the divine good for us is to refuse to receive God's love and to refuse to extend God's love in us to others. Thomas begins his account of spiritual indifference with a reference to charity or love (Thomas's *caritas* is closer to our English word *love* than it is to our *charity*, though it is far richer than either); thus, his discussion returns me to my opening puzzlement about how my thoughts of the reactions of others to my death transformed itself into thoughts of my reaction to their deaths. Thomas makes it clear that spiritual indifference is resistance to one's divinely given vocation as creature created by love and for love. And because it is resistance against God — because it is an act of a creature's will against God, precisely as God is present with that creature — spiritual indifference is sinful in the most fundamental way. It is, in fact, the very essence of sin, for it is the will to be radically *alone*, born of a fearfulness of relationship. Death threatens us with isolation, and we fantasize about our relationships with others as compensation. To be shaken out of such spiritual indifference is to be rocked by the horrors of genuine loneliness but also reassured by the intimations of one's true relatedness.

Memory has reminded me of loneliness and compensatory efforts at self-assurance; it has also suggested less illusory assurance. Unlike Thoreau, I have not looked upon a river in a meditative hour and been reminded of the flux of all things, but when I was about fourteen years old, I did look outside a car window upon a sordid little strip mall — with people scurrying back and forth in pursuit of the countless trivialities of their petty, insignificant lives — and I was, for a few moments, so utterly overwhelmed by the value and significance in God's eyes of the ordinary lives that rushed passed me that tears flooded my own eyes (read Augustine's *Confessions* to discover how much tears — and the absence of tears — can reveal about the spiritual state of those who do not cry very often). Unlike Augustine, I have not responded to the sound of children chanting, "Take it and read, take it and read," but when I was about twenty years old, I did sit down one afternoon on a campus bench and casually open a news magazine — a story about a recent airline disaster jumped out at me, accompanied by a photograph that caught my full attention. The color photo was grainy, slightly blurred; someone with a loaded camera at hand had caught the airliner in its death dive, plunging at a nearly vertical angle, with the treetops visible in the lower third of the frame (my pulse quickens as this twenty-year-old memory returns; I see again in my mind's eye the sunlight glinting off the grainy metal fuselage). There they are — all one hundred plus passengers, frozen in time, a split second before their deaths. You can even see the plane's passenger windows; I look closely and squint, imagining I can see faces. And my throat tightens as I am overwhelmed with ... with ... sadness. Yes, *sadness* is just the right word. And suddenly I knew that God was, in that very moment before impact, also sad, with a sadness whose depth surpassed my imagination and revealed the shallowness of my own sadness. I also knew that God's grief was matched by God's care — that somehow, equally beyond my imagination, those people, nameless to me but not to God, were thoroughly encircled in hands whose embrace their deaths could never shake. And at my certainty — not of God's existence but of God's character —

I rejoiced. Like sadness, *rejoiced* is also the only right word, though frankly it is a word I rarely, if ever, use, except when mindlessly singing hymns.

Like Augustine, Thomas assures us that indifference about our spiritual lives is sorrow over (resistance to the joy of) our own highest good, God's goodness, which has always been for us and is already in us. Although spiritual indifference is resistance to love, it is also recognition of that resistance; although it is confrontation with loneliness, it is also passion for relationship. Our creaturely reality as beings created by love and intended for love, combined with our fallen state as sinners who refuse to love, makes spiritual indifference possible, and in its possibility lies its promise. Becoming less indifferent requires us to risk confronting ourselves to receive that promise. We must enter into ourselves and learn who we really are. And just who are we, really? Christians believe that individual identity is a consequence of creation and redemption in Christ. In the sacrament of baptism, non-Christians receive their "Christian names," which are the sign that baptism into the body of Christ's death confirms and confers the unique, individual identities of all who will rise with Christ. The introspection that can lead the fearful, isolated self to encounter the person named in baptism is a first step in the "following" of Christ, through death to resurrection. Such encounters will be traumatic, for there is an old self whose life we must claim as our own and whose death we must live. But Christians believe that this trauma was God's before it was humanity's. Christians believe that God in Christ has already been wounded and that such wounding mysteriously heals all the wounds that have already beset and will yet traumatize humanity, down to one's most personal, private loneliness and sense of divine abandonment (Jesus cries out on the cross, "My God, my God, why have you forsaken me?" (Matt. 27:46) Yet Paul affirms that the resurrected Christ "lives to God" (Rom. 6:10)). Ancient Christians recited often the following aphorism about the incarnation of God in Christ: "God became human so that human beings might become divine." Henri Nouwen's restatement in *Reaching Out* may capture better the gift of personal identity bestowed by God in Christ: "Jesus came to us to become as we are *and left us* to allow us to become as he is." Jesus now lives to God, and we have our lives only in him. Becoming as he is — encountering our lives as they are in him — will only begin for us when we recognize and enter more deeply into our spiritual indifference, which is a sign of our opposition to God, but more fundamentally a witness to our not-quite-extinguished desire for God.

Our Responsibility

Fear of the consequences of self-giving drives us into isolation, and when we are isolated in our loneliness, we do not respond but only react. As our plane descends, perhaps we will assess re-actions: How much will others grieve at losing us? How much would we grieve at losing them? Behind both questions lurks a deep suspicion that we may not have a selfhood sufficient to grieve or worthy of being grieved over. Like Binx Bolling, the protagonist of Walker Percy's *The Moviegoer*, we sometimes sense that we are riddled with vacuoles — like vaguely poly-morphic amoebae, we draw within ourselves whatever promises to fill us up. Those outside who, we think, supply what we lack become our authorities, those who reject our pleas become our enemies, and those who seem to promise but finally fail to fill our needs become our disappointments. Family members often disappoint one another in just this latter way, by implic-itly holding out promises of fulfillment that no person should ever expect from another. We all know children whose parents "have not met their needs," parents whose children have "dis-appointed" them, brothers and sisters who have "failed" one another.

While our contemporary American culture pushes us into various forms of all-too-real competitive individualism, at the same moment it taunts us with utopian, guilt-engendering images of harmonious communal life and family togetherness. Prime-time television currently gives us intensely competitive lawyers, police officers, and trauma surgeons, back-to-back with saccharine sitcoms, in which provisionally frustrated fam-ily or love relationships are rewoven into rewarding wholes (with or without angelic aid), and all serious inner needs are fi-

nally satisfied in the most amusingly unexpected ways. Popular
culture diverts us with plenty of isolated individuals and warm
and fuzzy fantasy families; what it does not offer (because they
rarely exist, or because they are perceived to be boring?) are
fully centered persons who, knowing who they really are, can
then reach out in loving response toward others to build authentic communities. The Christian tradition calls such persons
saints, and nowadays they seem few and far between.

Becoming less indifferent about our spiritual lives requires
that we expose the illusions of our lives and the falseness of our
identities. Illusion and falsehood are exposed just to the extent
that our innermost identities are discerned. Only when we are
centered and secure as the persons who we really are, can we
then extend ourselves fearlessly in responsiveness and responsibility to others. Until we have entered into our own unique
hearts and encountered ourselves as persons with distinct and
valued identities *unlike* the identities of all others, we will be
unable to regard other people as truly different from ourselves,
seeing them instead merely as ways of satisfying our own needs,
as potential aspects of our own as-yet-incomplete personhood.
Let us just observe ourselves in ordinary, casual conversation.
How often do we really respond to what the other person says
to us, and how often do we react to what is said by selecting
some aspect of the other's remark that satisfies some need of
our own, especially a need that we have already allowed external authorities to define? Most of our conversation consists of
doing just this, cleverly disguised as taking an interest in other
people. It is rare to find someone who will listen to what we
say without using it at once as an occasion to satisfy his or her
own need. And, though we really do have the best intentions,
we rarely listen to others either.

My son is at his T-ball game. He has hit the ball and is standing on first base. The next batter hits the ball, and my son takes
off — not for second base, but for the ball — he has momentarily forgotten that he's playing offense, not defense. The coach
has not forgotten, however — he yells at my son, then, at the
first opportunity, strides out in the field to say something I cannot hear. When the inning is over, my son comes off the field
in tears, barely able to choke out his explanation. I recount this

painful moment not to indict the coach for insensitivity but to remind myself of the first impulse that shot through my mind: the urge to side with the coach and chide my son for not "keeping his head in the game." Why *that* impulse — and not that other instinct ("left over from the greatness of our original nature") to console an obviously distraught child? Because at that moment I was on the brink of losing myself by letting others — the coach, the other parents — simultaneously define and satisfy my own need to be well-regarded by them: after all, how could I be well regarded if I am the father of a boy who could not even realize he was supposed to run to second base instead of field the ball? Fortunately, I suppressed this impulse to join in ritualized criticism and responded instead with consolation. But I do not regard my moment of temptation lightly. Every week I go to these games, and every week the field is surrounded by parents — predominantly males — who, by the commands and criticisms they so readily bark out, use their children as means to the end of meeting their own need to be well regarded by others (even though, if challenged, they will say — and really mean it — that they are only helping their children become better players and enjoy the game more).

Our children or our students or our close family members provide a litmus test for whether we are centered persons in our own right who no longer look to others to satisfy our needs, and whose needs are no longer defined by the regard of those outside us. At the milder end of the spectrum, we call such use of those close to us *bad parenting*, *bad teaching*, or *dysfunctional family life*. At the other end of the spectrum, we label such relationships *abusive*. They can and do often end in violence. When the circle of persons involved is wider, our reactive rather than responsive relationships become charged with larger consequences; our failure to discover a selfhood capable of being shared rather than filled becomes a social and political and not simply personal event. Rather than consisting of responsive actions born out of our innermost identities, our lives can become collections of passive reactions to whatever impinges on us, claims our attention, and promises to bestow value on who we are or what we do.

To be spiritually indifferent means to accept a reactive mode of life, to retreat from responsiveness into social and political paralysis. One great benefit of a television remote control is that it lets us click quickly past the many horrific images of human evil and suffering that the evening news throws into our laps, as though we were supposed to do something about them. In *Sources of the Self*, the philosopher Charles Taylor has observed that we find ourselves paralyzed by such images, not because we disagree about the character or importance of justice and benevolence, but because we lack the strong "sources" that could "support our far-reaching moral commitments." Taylor understands that commitments to justice and benevolence unsupported by deep sources bring evil in their wake:

> High standards need strong sources. This is because there is some-thing morally corrupting, even dangerous, in sustaining the de-mand simply on the feeling of undischarged obligation, on guilt, or its obverse, self-satisfaction. Hypocrisy is not the only neg-ative consequence. Morality as benevolence on demand breeds self-condemnation for those who fall short and a depreciation of the impulses to self-fulfillment, seen as so many obstacles raised by ego-ism to our meeting the standard. . . . If morality can only be powered negatively, where there can be no such thing as beneficence powered by an affirmation of the recipient as a being of value, then pity is destructive to the giver and degrading to the receiver, and the ethic of benevolence may indeed be indefensible.

A return to the sources that could foster and sustain acts of benevolence and justice will not happen apart from a return to the true center of our own personhood. Responding to others as different and worthy of full regard in themselves rather than reacting to them only because they can satisfy our own needs requires that we first know and accept who we really are. For Christians, who we really are is defined by our creation by God in Christ. But knowing who we really are as creatures created and redeemed in Christ and living our lives out of our own cen-ter in Christ requires us *to live out a reality* and not simply learn and repeat a theological truth.

The discontent that signals recognition of one's spiritual in-difference is the first stirring of prayer. Prayer is the movement from reactive isolation to self-giving responsiveness to others, to God and to other persons. In the Christian tradition, this movement is understood to be a gift, indeed, the very activity

of God within oneself: "You stir us to take pleasure in praising
you," writes Augustine. Or as Paul declares to the Christians in
Rome: "the Spirit helps us in our weakness; for we do not know
how to pray as we ought, but the Spirit himself intercedes for
us with sighs too deep for words" (Rom. 8:26). Sitting around
avoiding prayer by wondering how to pray or contemplating
(only to reject) various silly or manipulative forms of pseudo-
prayer are just the peculiar "spiritual" forms of diversion likely
to appeal to religiously minded persons. Meanwhile, prayer is
already underway, made visible when our discontent surfaces
and we attend to, rather than suppress evidence of, our restlessness. I have avoided up to this point any direct mention of
prayer because . . . well . . . it's a topic I like to avoid. Or evade. I
find particularly annoying the remark of the fourth-century her-
mit and expert on acedia Evagrius of Pontus: "A theologian is
one whose prayer is true." Yet this essay has, probably despite
itself, concerned our first, stumbling, inchoate recognitions of
prayer, and it has sought to cultivate forms of attention that
can lead us to perceive and enter into that prayer that is already
underway within us. Through the invocation of memory and
the invitation to memory, I have been calling us to responsiveness, first to what we can discern about ourselves if only we will
turn within and then to that extended responsiveness to others
in self-giving that is the heart of our larger social and political
responsibility.

Do I think that such responsiveness can authentically emerge
for Christians apart from the attentive reading of Scripture informed by the diverse witness of the Christian tradition and the
full engagement of human reason or in isolation from the corporate life of Christians in the church? Certainly not. Do I think
that Christian introspection and meditative self-knowledge can
occur apart from Christ, the image of God according to which
Christians believe they are created and redeemed? Certainly not.
Do I doubt for one moment that there is a profound, life-
endangering difference between the quick-fix anodynes of much
contemporary care-of-soul therapy and the rich and subtle traditions of Christian meditation and contemplation, informed by
Scripture and tradition? Not for a minute. What I do know
is that there is a profound, life-endangering difference between

holding Christian views, however orthodox, on all such matters and allowing them to inform one's own life as lived from day to day. Many of us, within the Christian church and on its periphery, understand this difference intuitively and will not mistake unlived theology for valid prayer, even if some of us are sure we do not know how to pray (or do not want to) or profess not to have a clue as to what theologians think about. This essay is not a plea for more praying or more theologizing (Christians will, in any case, already be doing both); it is an invitation to enter into and embrace our spiritual indifference as both witness and responsibility. For to recognize oneself as spiritually indifferent is already to have moved — to have been moved — beyond sheer indifference that surely is death-in-life and to have been invited to respond in self-giving love to oneself, to others, and to that larger "life eternal" that is everlasting because it is the character of real life always to be alive.

Taking the train in lieu of the backup flight to Boston that day obliged me to return to Philadelphia by the same means. I had sat by myself on the trip up, alone with the ruminations already described. As it turned out, a former teacher, also traveling alone, asked if he might return together with me until his stop. So we talked at length about all manner of things, picking up where we had last left our joint transformation of a former student-teacher relationship into newly evolving colleagueship and ever-deepening friendship. Of course, death was now far, far from my mind; after all, the plane had landed safely, and my recent experience had already provided especially good material for diverting cocktail repartee. I was immortal once again. After my companion had disembarked, I thought for some time about our ongoing relationship and the ways it would surely change and grow richer over the coming years. But before the new year was over, I would return for his funeral. And then I would grieve, and not just imagine to grieve, for the death of another. Then I would, amidst the company of the gathered community, set aside for a while my illusions of immortality and hope instead for the resurrection of the body and the life everlasting.

For Further Reading

Classic Christian Writings on Spirituality

Augustine. *Confessions.* Translated with an introduction and notes by Henry Chadwick. New York: Oxford University Press, 1991. Especially Books 1–9.

Pascal, Blaise. *Pensées.* Translated with an introduction by A. J. Krailsheimer. New York: Viking Penguin, 1966. Especially the section entitled "Diversion."

Reflective Writings on Christian Spirituality

Leech, Kenneth. *True Prayer: An Invitation to Christian Spirituality.* San Francisco: Harper & Row, 1980. A richly detailed historically and thematically organized examination of traditional Christian reflections on prayer.

Norris, Kathleen. *The Cloister Walk.* New York: Riverhead Books, 1996. See especially the chapter on *acedia.* Firsthand experiences with contemporary practices of traditional Christian monastic life.

Nouwen, Henri J. M. *Reaching Out: the Three Movements of the Spiritual Life.* New York: Doubleday, 1975. Personally framed reflections by leading student and practitioner of Christian spirituality, focusing on the social and ethical dimensions of Christian spiritual experience.

Scholarly Studies

Kuhn, Reinhard. *The Demon of Noontide: Ennui in Western Literature.* Princeton: Princeton University Press, 1976. Wide ranging and detailed exploration of ennui in classic literary texts.

Spacks, Patricia Meyer. *Boredom: The Literary History of a State of Mind.* Chicago and London: University of Chicago Press, 1995. Reflections on boredom as a theme in modern and contemporary literature.

Taylor, Charles. *Sources of the Self: The Making of Modern Identity.* Cambridge, Mass.: Harvard University Press, 1989. Exploration of Western literary and philosophical texts by a contemporary philosopher seeking to uncover the deep commitments and evasions that have shaped modern identity.

Wenzel, Siegfried. *The Sin of Sloth: Acedia in Medieval Thought and Literature.* Chapel Hill: University of North Carolina Press, 1967. Scholarly examination of the place of acedia in traditional Christian thought and practice.

3

WHY DO THE INNOCENT SUFFER?

Thomas F. Tracy

The Book of Job tells us that when Job's friends hear of his great misfortune, they come to visit in the hope of offering some comfort. They find him in terrible condition — his children dead, his wealth gone, his body covered with festering boils. His wife is repelled by his stench, the neighbors turn from him in disgust, and village children stare at him with horror. He sits outdoors alone, scraping the pus from his wounds with a shard of broken pottery and grieving for his lost children, his lost way of life, his lost confidence in God's favor and benevolence toward him.

This is an arresting picture of human suffering, and we can imagine the alarm that Job's friends must feel when they first come upon him. No doubt they would have seen such misery before among the ever-present poor on the margins of their society, but this was one of their own, a man renowned both for his wealth and his piety. They are appalled at what Job has suffered, and they feel compelled to respond in some way, both to support him and to make sense of his terrible misfortune.

Like Job's friends, we may be shocked by the depth of suffering in our world when we are brought to look it in the face. If we are lucky, we do not know personally what it is like to experience the sorts of accumulating calamities that turned Job's life upside down. But we can hardly avoid being witnesses to profound human misery, whether close at hand or only at a distance. Life inevitably includes painful losses, and when we acknowledge this to each other and tell our stories, we discover that we belong to a much larger community of grief. In addition, the modern media flood us with information about other people's suffering, turning us into "bystanders" at many of the world's most dramatic tragedies and injustices. Newspapers and television vividly (often luridly) deliver each day's bad news, and if we pay even a little attention, the litany of sorrows may threaten to overwhelm us.

As a result, we too feel the need to make sense of the presence of apparently arbitrary suffering and loss in a world made by God. This is not an easy thing to do, and our attempts may go wrong in a variety of ways, as Job's conversation with his friends makes clear. Their attempts to explain Job's suffering lead them to condemn him rather than to comfort him. It is worthwhile to think about why this happens, particularly since their strategy of explanation is so familiar and deeply rooted. I want to suggest another way of thinking about these issues than that pursued by Job's friends, but this will require that we acknowledge some important limits on our ability to give reasons for human suffering.

The first thing to notice about the response of Job's friends to his predicament is that it begins in silence. They are stunned by the misery that has overtaken him, and they simply sit near him, uttering not a word but keeping company with him in his sorrows. For seven days they manage to resist the familiar urge to "say something," and this respectful silence is not broken until Job himself finally speaks. When he does, his words are painful for his friends to hear; from the depths of his bitter anguish Job curses the day of his own birth:

> God damn the day I was born
>   and the night that forced me from the womb.
> On that day — let there be darkness;
>   let it never have been created;
>   let it sink back into the void.
> . . . .
> If only I had strangled or drowned
>   on my way to the bitter light.
>
>   (Mitchell, p. 13; cf. Job 3:2–3, 12–13)*

Here is the measure of Job's misery. He mourns not just his many losses; he also laments having lived at all. His life has

---

*Note that subsequent references to the Mitchell translation will appear with page number only.

become an intolerable burden for him, and he longs for death, he says, "as if it were buried treasure" (p. 14; Job 3:21).

One of the ironies of traditional interpretation is that Job has been presented as a model of patience in suffering. This may be apt as a description of the character in the ancient folktale retold in the prose prologue (chaps. 1–2) and epilogue (42:7–17) of the Book of Job. But the folktale only provides the stage setting for a much deeper and more searching discussion, in poetic form, of suffering and injustice (3:1–42:6). I will focus exclusively upon this poetic dialogue, in which Job is nothing if not noisy and tenacious in stating his complaint against the injustice of what has happened to him. Precisely because he understands his life as lived before God, he raises his voice to God in protest. He pours the passion of his suffering *and* his faith into a profound and persistent questioning of God's ways.

The issue that Job now confronts "in person" is a perennial stumbling block for any monotheism. If there is but one ultimate power at the foundation of all things, then the fact of evil in the world calls God's goodness in question. This difficulty has been expressed by philosophers in the form of a dilemma. If God is altogether good, then God has the *motive* to eliminate evil. If God is all-powerful, then God has the *means* to eliminate evil. So why is there evil in the world? Job does not, of course, raise this question simply as an interesting puzzle, an abstract problem created by pointing to suffering he has not experienced in order to challenge a faith he does not share. On the contrary, this issue arises for him as an urgent spiritual and physical crisis. Job himself, in his longing for an end to the existence that God has given him, becomes the principal piece of evidence entered in his case against the justice of God's governance of the world.

Once Job has broken the silence, the dialogue with his friends can begin, and it is by no means a sedate exchange of theological opinion. All of the parties to this conversation have a great deal at stake in it, and as often happens with matters about which we care deeply, the discussion quickly becomes heated. With some variation in emphasis, Job's three friends all put forward essentially the same view — a view we can call the *theodicy of retribution*. Theodicies offer a moral justification of God's permitting suffering and evil in the world. The justification offered by Job's friends begins with two convictions: (1) God is just. (2) Justice requires that no one suffer unless he or she deserves to suffer. These both seem to be reasonable beliefs, but it follows immediately from them that (3) if you are suffering, you must have done something to deserve it. Their dilemma, when confronted with Job's predicament, is that they must either give up one of their fundamental convictions or make a case that Job has sinned and, in fact, is a sinner of such magnitude that he deserves to be sitting in the dust scraping his boils with broken pottery. They choose to make the best (or worst) they can of the second alternative, and each of them tries out various strategies of argument.

Eliphaz begins by reminding Job that God is unapproachably holy, so that not even the angels can withstand God's searching gaze. We should not be surprised if God finds fault with us, therefore, but simply accept the divine chastisement and ask forgiveness for whatever unknown offense we may have given. Bildad tries a less subtle approach, but one that was well-entrenched in tradition. He contends that if the fault does not lie with Job himself (and it is clear that he thinks it does), then it must lie with Job's children, who no doubt deserved what they got and, by implication, dragged Job down with them. It is not difficult to imagine how this bit of conventional wisdom might sound to Job, whose grief over the deaths of his children would be as raw as his open wounds. The third speaker, Zophar, returns to the basic argument pursued throughout the dialogue by all three comforters. Surely, he says, Job must at least have committed some secret inner transgression. If God were to make plain Job's innermost motivations and hidden purposes, then the sin for which he suffers would be evident. "Come now," he says, "repent of your sins. . . . Then your soul will be pure; . . . All your suffering will vanish" (p. 32; Job 11:13–16).

There are three rounds of this discussion, with each friend successively making his case and Job in turn replying. Relatively little is added in the later rounds to this basic array of arguments. But as the discussion progresses, the three friends become increasingly alarmed at the boldness of Job's resistance to their traditional religious views, and so they add a further sin to their list: the sin of stubbornly insisting upon his own innocence and questioning the justice of God. The attitude he displays in this very discussion, they say, provides ample reason for God to punish him. Eliphaz gives particularly vivid expression to this view:

> Does a wise man spout such nonsense
> and fill his belly with gas?
> Does he blurt out useless arguments,
> words that can do no good?
> You are undermining religion
> and crippling faith in God.
> Sin has seduced your mind;
> your tongue flaps with deceit.
> Your mouth condemns you, not I;
> your own lips testify against you.

(p. 41; Job 15:2–6)

At this point, the friends who came to offer comfort have instead become accusers. They are driven to this angry confrontation by their refusal to budge from the inference that, since God is good, suffering must be distributed according to a principle of justice that we can discern.

Job steadfastly resists this view, insisting that the world does not work in the way his friends suggest. He tenaciously holds to a truth that he now knows in his own person and sees confirmed in the world around him: namely, that innocent persons suffer terribly. At the same time, injustice often goes unchecked, and the wicked grow powerful and arrogant in their wrongdoing. Consider Job's vivid description of the plight of the poor.

> The poor, like herds of cattle,
> wander across the plains,
> searching all day for food,
> picking up scraps for their children.
> Naked, without a refuge,
> they shiver in the bitter cold.
> When it rains, they are drenched to the bone;
> they huddle together in caves.
> They carry grain for the wicked
> and break their backs for the rich.
> They press olives and starve,
> crush grapes and go thirsty.

(p. 60; Job 24:5–11)

The theodicy of retribution flies in the face of the facts; God does not run the world as a system of rewards and punishments. It is remarkable that even as Job questions God's justice, he appeals to God to vindicate the truth of his words. Job's friends refuse to acknowledge the evident facts about social injustice and the suffering of the innocent because to do so would complicate their theology. Their resistance to this truth amounts to a kind of cover-up on God's behalf, and that is something God will not abide:

> Will you lie to vindicate God?
>   Will you perjure yourselves for him?
> Will you blindly stand on his side,
>   pleading his case alone?
> What will you do when he questions you?
>   Can you cheat him as you would a man?
> Won't he judge you severely
>   if your testimony is false?

(pp. 34–35; Job 13:7–10)

Job trusts that God is a partisan of truth and will prefer honest moral questioning to a disingenuous defense. It is important to emphasize that Job turns out to be *right* about this. At the end of the poetic dialogue, after the divine voice has spoken from the whirlwind, God expresses displeasure at the three friends because they have not "spoken the truth about me, as my servant Job has" (p. 91; Job 42:7).

It is worth noting another powerful objection to the theodicy of retribution. This view blames the sufferer for his suffering, and so quite literally adds insult to injury. In addition to the physical burden of his boils, Job must (on this view) carry a moral burden of guilt and a social burden of public identification as a wicked man. The theology of retribution may vindicate God's justice, but it does so by convicting the sufferer. It justifies and legitimates misery; after all, Job only gets what he deserves. And this breaks solidarity with the sufferer, distinguishing him or her as a sinner from the rest of us who apparently are doing better. It is no accident that the theology of retribution is most likely to be championed by people who are (at least for the time being) pleased with their lives.

Job's lament includes grief and anger at this failure of compassion in friends who cling to their explanation of suffering
even though it means that they must repudiate the sufferer: "My
friends are streams that go dry, riverbeds in the desert.... You
too have turned against me; my wretchedness fills you with
fear" (p. 22; Job 6:15, 21). Suffering frightens us, and we typically respond by looking for differences between ourselves and
the sufferer. If you are in some way responsible for your misfortune, then I can hope to avoid what has befallen you. I can
explain why you suffer as you do (and, by implication, why I do
not), and in this way I can avoid admitting the unsettling fact
that you and I are alike in our vulnerability. The price of compassion is acknowledgment of this unwelcome truth, and so we
often draw back physically and morally from the one who suffers, as though suffering is contagious and can be avoided if we
keep a safe distance. As a result, part of the sting of suffering
is loneliness:

> All my friends have forgotten me;
>   my neighbors have thrown me away.
> My relatives look through me
>   as though I didn't exist.
> . . . .
> My dearest friends despise me;
>   I have lost everyone I love.
>
> (pp. 48–49; Job 19:13–14, 19)

The theodicy of retribution provides a religious rationale for
this isolation, and that is another reason to reject it.

The net effect of the attempt by Job's friends to explain his
suffering is that they have added to his wounds and deepened
his sorrows. The neat structure of their theodicy cannot accommodate the challenge presented by his experience, and so
they sacrifice compassion in order to preserve a familiar theory.
One of the ironies of the story of Job is that his friends offer
their most articulate response to his misery precisely when they
simply sit with him and say nothing.

The theodicy of retribution fails, in part, because it tries to
explain too much. Job's friends thought that they needed to
spell out the purpose of Job's misfortune. By contrast, I want to
suggest that we cannot expect to provide a detailed explanation

of why individuals face particular hardships. One reason for this is relatively simple; we usually do not know enough about the relevant circumstances to say exactly what purposes might be served by specific evils. Beyond this, I will defend a further, more controversial claim. Sometimes the misfortunes we suffer simply do not have a purpose for us; that is, they cannot be explained as the *means* to some greater good. When we affirm that God can bring good out of evil, this does not mean that every evil that befalls us, no matter how terrible, is sent by God for our own good (whether as punishment for sin or a test of faith or some other improvement of our character). To put it simply, people suffer in ways that are in fact bad for them. When this harm nonetheless leads to the emergence of some good in the sufferer's life, this is a work of grace that redeems and heals, rather than an outcome built into a means/ends strategy.

If this is correct, then it will come as no surprise that the type of theodicy put forward by Job's friends does not succeed and, in fact, only deepens our perplexity about evil. We may be able to say some things about why, in general, God permits the sorts of evils we see around us, but we should not expect always to see a purpose for particular evils. Our explanations of evil will have to remain sketchy, and rather than trying to figure out in each case *why God permits evil*, it will be more important to focus upon *what God does to overcome it*.

In order for us to see this more clearly, it will help to look at one familiar way of explaining why a God of perfect love and free creative power would bring into being a world that includes the sorts of evils we find around us. Attempts to justify God's permission of evil typically point to some very great good that cannot be achieved, even by God, without allowing evil. The challenge is (1) to identify this good and (2) to explain, at least in general terms, the relation of various evils to it.

A great deal depends upon how we understand the good purposes that require God's permission of evil. Many modern discussions have focused on the value of human freedom, moral responsibility, and moral growth. These are undoubtedly important, but according to Christianity, a life of moral depth and integrity is not the *highest* good that God makes available to us. The fullest meaning of our lives is found in fellowship with

God, as God meets us in the humanity of Jesus and confirms
us in this relationship through the work of the Spirit. The God
whose very being is loving relationship creates us for the sake
of such a relationship. Our moral freedom has value because
it plays a role in making us what we are, namely, the kind of
creatures who can stand in this distinctively *personal* relationship to God. In addition, communion with God is a good that
includes and transcends the span of our biological lifes; Christian faith looks in hope toward life with God beyond death. We
need not suppose that the divine-human relationship is the only
good God pursues in creation; if creation is good, then it was
good throughout the vast cosmic history before our species appeared in this tiny corner of a spiral galaxy. But we can glimpse
God's wider purposes in creation only by reflecting on the good
in which we participate.

Given this understanding of God's good purposes, what can
we say about why the world includes the evils we lament? In
creating us, God brings into being a creature that must have a
particular sort of history, namely, a history of personal relationships in which we become who we are in a community of other
persons. It appears that this is possible only under conditions
that also make possible various evils.

Consider, in the first place, the moral dimension of our relationships with one another. Moral life requires that we be able
to recognize and reflect on questions about right and wrong,
about values, and about what is fair and just. It also requires
that we be able to act upon our judgments, living out the consequences of our choices. This opens up the possibility that we will
make wrong moral choices as well as right ones and that we will
do significant harm to ourselves and others. I noted above that
moral reflection and action are not the highest good for which
God makes us. But the capacity for moral life is an essential part
of being a person in community with other persons. If God is to
make creatures like us, then God must allow that we may choose
to do what we ought not to do. Moral evil, and the suffering
that it brings, is therefore attributed primarily to human beings
and only indirectly to the God who called us into being.

This is commonly known as the *free-will* reply to the problem of evil, and it has received a great deal of discussion. The

appeal to human moral freedom provides one way of explaining why innocent people suffer; namely, they are victims of other people's morally wrong choices. It also helps make clear why we should hesitate to say that suffering can always be explained in terms of its good purpose for the sufferer. When one person's actions harm another, it is possible that this might turn out to be the best means to the sufferer's own good. But it certainly appears that this is not always the case; consider the innocents who perished at Auschwitz or in the bombing of Dresden or in the streets of Sarajevo. If we were to say that all innocent suffering at the hands of others is for the sufferer's own good, it would lead to some unacceptable conclusions. For example, it would mean that all victims of injustice, no matter how terrible their mistreatment, are best off suffering just as they do. Job's friends insisted that Job deserved his misery; this view would add that if he did not deserve it, he in any case *needed* it. Even the worst human injustices then become unwitting contributions to a divinely orchestrated scheme of correction or education, a vast pedagogy of pain. Further, this view would make it difficult to explain what is wrong with hurting other people. If we thought that God would permit us to harm others only when doing so is for their own good, it would be fair to ask why we should refrain (or even if it is wrong *not* to harm them).

The problem with such a theodicy is that it gives suffering *too much* meaning; moral evil is incorporated into God's purposes in such a way that it is legitimated and loses its character as "that which ought not to be." If we reject this type of theodicy, however, then we must acknowledge that moral evils may be committed that are not necessary or best as the means to a greater good. Moral evils need not and ought not to be done, and the victims of our all-too-human inhumanity need not and ought not to suffer as they do. But if God is to create persons, then God must permit us to make morally significant choices. And though the evils that result are not required as a means to a good end, God can bring good out of them. This is the healing and redeeming work of God, which does not leave innocent suffering as a meaningless loss but rather incorporates and transforms these sorrows within the relationship that God fashions with the sufferer, a relationship grounded in God's act of entering into the midst of human suffering.

The free-will reply clearly is helpful in addressing questions about moral evils, but it appears to be of little use in explaining why we are subject to *natural evils*, the suffering that befalls us simply by virtue of being animals in the natural world. We might try to understand natural suffering as a consequence of sin, as did many premodern interpreters of the creation stories in Genesis. I will suppose, however, that these evils are an inherent part of the natural world God creates and so are not primarily attributable to human wrongdoing, though human choices will dramatically affect our exposure to them. What, then, can we say about natural suffering?

Here we need to take a further step in thinking about the conditions for our existence. We can discover and develop our various capacities as persons (e.g., our moral, cognitive, affective, and aesthetic powers) only if we exist within a stable and consistent natural environment. For example, the unfolding moral life that we just considered requires that we be able to assess alternative courses of action, calculate likely consequences, and act with a reasonable expectation of the result. A world in which events do not fall into reliable patterns would leave us unable to form an intelligible map of its structure and therefore unable to learn or to act. If, however, the world has a stable, lawful structure, then it will be possible for us to collide with it and to be hurt in the process.

The structures of nature must not only be reliable; they must also be impersonal and amoral. Imagine, for a moment, a world in which we knew that each person always received from nature exactly what she deserved, considered from a moral point of view. A self-serving lie, say, might merit a head cold (with more serious offenses receiving proportionally more severe punishments). Under these circumstances, a virtue like compassion would not make much sense; medical efforts to relieve physical suffering would both be morally questionable (as an attempt to circumvent just punishment) and be doomed to fail (until the moral problem was corrected). In a cosmic nursery school of this sort, we would be maintained in perpetual moral childhood, continually prodded by rewards and punishments and never allowed enough moral independence to develop an identity and integrity of character as a moral agent.

There are good reasons, then, why natural suffering is not distributed according to any moral rule that we can discern. If we are to acquire knowledge of our world and make moral choices within it, then we must live in a world in which it rains on the just and the unjust. We will have to take our chances in a natural environment that not only nurtures and sustains us but that also can destroy us, an environment that makes possible both flourishing and perishing. Natural suffering can serve as the means to various goods: for example, empathy and compassion, fortitude and endurance, self-examination and reassessment of our attachments. But we should not think of natural misfortune as invariably "sent" for such a purpose. That view generates the same sorts of problems we noted in considering the comparable suggestion about suffering at the hands of other persons. Sometimes bad things happen to us quite apart from whether we deserve them or need them in order to be taught some lesson. Natural evils occur as a side effect, or by-product, of making possible the existence of creatures like us, and so they may not always have an explanation in terms of some specific good that they make possible for the individual sufferer. What is needed in the face of such suffering is not theological explanation but compassion and, whenever possible, action that addresses the natural sources of suffering.

Much more needs to be said about both natural and moral evils than can be provided in this brief sketch. One question in particular deserves additional comment. It might be replied that although this account helps us to understand why God creates a world that includes *some* moral and natural evils, it does not explain why the world contains *so much* suffering from these sources. Perhaps there is far more suffering than God would need to allow in order to serve the good purposes that we have discussed. We might grant that in creating finite persons God must permit us both to make serious moral choices and to run significant risks in the natural world. But we might still wonder whether God's purposes could be achieved with less misery and destruction. It certainly appears that plenty of evils in the world could be eliminated without adverse effect.

This reply reflects the compelling principle that evils ought to be kept to a minimum. But it also makes some important assumptions. It supposes that we can make at least a rough estimate of how much evil would be the unavoidable minimum that God must allow in accomplishing the good of creation. And it claims that we are justified in concluding that this minimum has been exceeded. These assumptions do not hold up well under scrutiny. The key difficulty is that we are not in a position to make either of these judgments. It is not enough just to offer examples of terrible and apparently pointless evils and then appeal to our justifiable desire that they not have occurred. This intuitively plausible way of arguing is insufficient for two reasons.

First, even if the world does contain a minimum of evils (relative to the goods made possible within it), it will still appear to us to include evils God could readily eliminate. We have already seen that moral and natural evils must be permitted even when they do not serve as the means to a greater good; they are the result of creating a world in which creatures like us may exist. This means that any single instance of such an evil could be eliminated without the loss of a specific good outcome to which it leads. There may, as a result, be no principled reason for God to permit one natural or moral evil rather than some other that is just as bad. There will be a reason for God to permit evils of this type, but not necessarily for permitting this particular bad thing to happen. We cannot expect, therefore, to see any reason for many evils, considered individually. But it does not follow from this that God should eliminate them. On the contrary, since God's permission of moral and natural evils is a condition for our existence, it is we who must do what we can to prevent or ameliorate them.

Second, in order to assess whether the world includes more evil than a benevolent creator should permit, we would need to be considerably more godlike in our knowledge than we are. In particular, we would need to understand a great deal about what God is up to in creation (e.g., about God's purposes throughout the nonhuman universe). And we would need to understand the alternatives open to God in achieving these creative purposes. This obviously exceeds our grasp, and so our efforts to understand the place of evil in the design of the world should be qualified by a correspondingly profound cognitive humility.

Here the story of Job once again speaks eloquently. Job's discussion with his friends ends in a way that is unusual, even among theologians. God enters the conversation:

> Where were you when I planned the earth?
>   Tell me if you are so wise.
> Do you know who took its dimensions,
>   measuring its length with a cord?
> What were its pillars built on?
>   Who laid down its cornerstone,
> while the morning stars burst out singing
>   and the angels shouted for joy!

(p. 79; Job 38:4–7)

The poet who devised the speech from the whirlwind could not resist the opportunity for some divine sarcasm. God's speech, with its relentless cadence of rhetorical questions, might be read simply as a matter of "pulling rank" in order to silence Job. Taken this way, the response misses the point. Job has called out for justice, and it is morally obtuse to reply with an assertion of superior power that browbeats him into submission. But this clearly is not all that is going on here. Job's attention (and ours) has been sharply focused on his suffering and on the debate with his friends. When God speaks, the frame of reference vastly expands. The voice from the whirlwind conducts Job on a brief but overwhelming tour of the wonders and terrors of creation. Job is reminded of the time before humanity, the primordial time at the beginning of things, when the world was born in joy. The foundations of this creation, the elemental forces and structures of the world, lie far beyond our reach. The universe is a place of monumental energies operating on a scale that dwarfs human powers. And this world was not made for us alone; we are surrounded by other living expressions of the divine creativity, and they provide a spectacle of life more varied in form and habit than we could ever have dreamed. The world, in short, reflects the workings of a creative vitality that is not of our ken, a numinous energy that is not scaled to human expectations. We find ourselves in the midst of God's world, and we are in no position to say just why creation takes the form it does or to judge whether the whole enterprise was a good idea.

This reply from the whirlwind leaves Job speechless with wonder, and so the discussion that was preceded by silent compassion ends in silent awe. The "answer" Job receives does not provide a solution to the problem of evil. It points to an intrinsic goodness that shines though the strangeness and beauty of the world, but it also vividly reminds us of the limits of human understanding. We cannot expect to explain in detail how all of the evils we experience fit into the wider scheme of things; this lies beyond our grasp.

The attempt to understand why we suffer, then, must be an exercise in carefully working along the boundaries of our comprehension. I have suggested that we can say some useful things about why God's good purposes might require the permission of various types of evils. But the question of whether God could achieve these purposes without permitting so much evil is not one that we can answer by tallying up goods and evils and analyzing their relations. Confidence in God's goodness cannot be grounded in an assurance that we can state the reason for each instance of evil that occurs. Our efforts at theodicy, like those of Job's friends, go wrong when we forget this.

Christian trust in the benevolence of God finds its sources elsewhere — namely, in the narratives of God's redemptive action in history. The God whom we meet in the Christian stories is by no means simply a cosmic accountant who carefully calculates an optimal overall balance of goods attained versus evils permitted and who then tolerates evil and suffering as a collateral cost of creation. Beyond any such abstract scrupulousness, God takes the astonishing step of meeting us in the midst of the world's evils, sparing nothing in order to share the divine life with us. Christian faith proclaims that in the life, death, and resurrection of Christ, God acts to redeem us as doers and sufferers of evil by taking us into a relationship grounded in the triumph of love over suffering in God's own life. This relationship fully incorporates the hard facts of suffering and evil, promising to make the broken creature whole. This does not provide an explanation of the world's evils. Rather, it points toward God's presence even in the darkest extremities of loss and grief, and it affirms that none of the evils we have suffered or done can put us beyond the reach of God's love. Paul's Letter to the Romans contains the great classical expression of this Christian hope:

> For I am sure that neither death, nor life, nor angels, nor principalities, nor things present, nor things to come, nor powers, nor height, nor depth, nor anything else in all creation, will be able to separate us from the love of God in Christ Jesus our Lord. (Rom. 8:38–39)

For Further Reading

Adams, Robert and Marilyn, eds. *The Problem of Evil*. Oxford: Oxford University Press, 1990. An excellent anthology containing many of the best known philosophical essays on God and evil.

Augustine. *Confessions, Book VII*. Trans. Rex Warner. New York: New American Library, 1963. The classic statement of the view that evil is not an entity or power in its own right but rather a disruption of God's good creation.

Berkovits, Eliezer. *Faith After the Holocaust*. New York: KTAV Publishing House, 1971. A subtle exploration of the resources available in Jewish tradition for understanding "God's terrible silence during the holocaust" (p. 85).

Davis, Stephen T., ed. *Encountering Evil: Live Options in Theodicy*. Atlanta: John Knox Press, 1981. A lively exchange in which the authors respond to one another's views on the justification of God's permission of evil.

Hick, John. *Evil and the God of Love*, rev. ed. San Francisco: Harper & Row, 1978. A highly influential contemporary theodicy that argues for the inevitable occurrence of evils in the process of human moral and spiritual growth.

Howard-Snyder, Daniel. *The Evidential Argument from Evil*. Bloomington: Indiana University Press, 1996. A collection of philosophical essays debating the question of whether the amounts and kinds of evil in the world provide sufficient evidence against the existence of God.

McGill, Arthur C. *Suffering: a Test of Theological Method*. Philadelphia: Westminster, 1982. A rich theological meditation on suffering that places at the center of the discussion God's radically self-giving life within the Trinity.

Mitchell, Stephen, trans. *The Book of Job*. San Francisco: North Point Press, 1987. A vivid modern translation.

Surin, Kenneth. *Theology and the Problem of Evil*. Oxford: Basil Blackwell, 1986. A sustained critique of the ways modern philosophers of religion have approached the problem of evil, and a call to refocus the discussion of the theology of the cross.

4

Is Jesus Christ the Unique
Mediator of Salvation?

J. A. Di Noia

Is Jesus Christ the unique mediator of salvation? The First Letter to Timothy provides an explicit answer: "There is one God, and there is one mediator between God and men, the man Christ Jesus, who gave himself as a ransom for all" (1 Tim 2:5). In the Acts of the Apostles, Saint Peter also gives a straightforwardly affirmative response to this question when he says, "There is salvation in no one else, for there is no other name under heaven given among men by which we must be saved" (Acts 4:12).

Despite the directness of these and other passages of Scripture, Christians have become increasingly reluctant to answer our question with a resounding affirmative. This reluctance arises in part from a desire to avoid giving offense to religious people of other traditions. To ascribe a uniquely salvific role to Jesus Christ would constitute a denial of the salvific role of other religious founders (like the Buddha and Muhammad) and thus would be an affront to their communities.

But a more seriously theological motivation for the reluctance to call Jesus the unique mediator of salvation is to avoid giving offense to God. The passage from 1 Timothy quoted above follows immediately after the statement that God "desires all men to be saved and to come to the knowledge of the truth" (1 Tim 2:4). To state that Christ possesses this role uniquely and, by implication, that only through faith in him can the salvation he mediates be attained seems to impose limits on what God plans to do and, moreover, what God can do. If it is as true now as it has been in the past that countless persons do not know or believe in Christ, then countless persons must fail to benefit from the salvation he uniquely mediates. In that case, God's plan of salvation as well as its execution would seem to be deficient in some radically unacceptable way.

Christians have struggled with our question for a long time, and as might be expected, they have come up with a range of ingenious responses to it. Today, our awareness of the value of other religious traditions and of the obvious goodness of many of their adherents renders the question all the more pressing.

The way that many theologians think about the issue today has been influenced by the pluralist theology of religions popularized by John Hick, Paul Knitter, and others. Pluralists claim, in a nutshell, that in one way or another all religions aim at salvation. In John Hick's influential definition, salvation is the movement from self-centeredness to "Reality-centeredness." Since, according to pluralists, ultimate Reality is incomprehensible and ineffable, no one religious description can claim primacy over rival descriptions, and no tradition can claim exclusive rights to the means of salvation. In the pluralist perspective, therefore, each religious founder must be regarded as in some sense a savior. Exclusive or unique status with respect to the knowledge of, provision for, or access to salvation can no more be claimed for Jesus of Nazareth than it can be claimed for Gautama the Buddha or for Muhammad. Naturally, pluralists do not deny that these founders were unique historical personalities. What they deny is that any one of them could provide a uniquely privileged or exclusive access to salvation.

It follows for pluralists that Christian theologians cannot give a simple affirmative answer to the question, Is Jesus Christ the unique mediator of salvation? On the basis of their study of religious traditions, pluralist philosophers and theologians contend that salvation, though diversely mediated, is nonetheless universally accessible. It is not just in order to avoid giving offense to other religious people that pluralists have championed this view. Pluralists argue on empirical and philosophical grounds that a soteriological structure underlies all religious traditions and thus variously orients their adherents to "Reality" as it is diversely figured in these traditions. Only in this way can

Christian theologians affirm the universality of salvation and of religious truth, at least as possibilities, without giving offense to other religious people.

To be sure, pluralists are not the only theologians who have been concerned with the salvation of persons who are not Christians. According to the typology prevailing in current theology of religions, the chief alternative positions on this issue are represented by exclusivism and inclusivism. In contrast to pluralists, both exclusivists and inclusivists would have no difficulty in giving an affirmative answer to the question, Is Jesus Christ the unique mediator of salvation? For all their sharp differences, exclusivists and inclusivists concur in their avowal of the uniquely salvific role of Christ. But exclusivists deny the possibility of salvation for non-Christians who do not before death explicitly profess faith in Christ. Inclusivists, on the other hand, allow for the possibility of salvation chiefly on the grounds of some form of implicit faith in Christ, combined with a morally upright life, on the part of non-Christians.

The Christian concern not to give offense to other religious people is a praiseworthy one, while the concern to allow for the possibility of their salvation is a doctrinally crucial one. But suppose that, far from being an affront to other religious traditions, a strong Christian affirmation of the uniqueness of Christ's salvific role is fundamental to traditional Christian universalism. Suppose, in other words, that the particularity of salvation in Christ is nonexclusive. Suppose, further, that an affirmation of this nonexclusive particularity of salvation in Christ is not an obstacle to but a condition for genuine respect for other religious people.

This position rests not only on central Christian doctrines but also on the suggestion that salvation is not a term that encompasses what all religions seek. It is a properly Christian designation for that which should be sought above all else in life. Salvation has a distinctively Christian content: transformation in Christ with a view to ultimate communion with the Triune God. Even where other religious communities employ the term salvation, their conceptions of the aim of life differ from one another and from that espoused by Christian communities. By framing the issues primarily in terms of the possibility of extra-Christian salvation, pluralists and inclusivists often fail to give enough weight to the distinctiveness of the goals religions aim at attaining. Inclusivists fail to notice their distinctiveness because they tend to reinterpret non-Christian patterns and aims in Christian terms. More at the center of attention here, however, are pluralists who make salvation an all-encompassing designation for the variety of aims that religious traditions espouse and commend.

If the issues at stake were framed differently, it might turn out that to affirm Christ's unique role in salvation is not to exclude persons who are not Christians but to embrace them. In other words, it might turn out that we could give a strong affirmative answer to the question, Is Jesus Christ the unique mediator of salvation? and still both show respect for other religious people and include them in the final consummation of all things for which we have reason, only in Christ, to hope.

In order to reframe these issues, and at the same time to identify what seems to be the weakness especially of typical pluralist approaches to them, let us engage in an experiment. Let us compare the question, Is Jesus Christ the unique mediator of salvation? with the question, Is the Buddha the unique revealer of the dharma? Suppose that I pose this second question to a Buddhist friend. Along with most other Buddhists, she will almost certainly answer it affirmatively. The dharma comprises all that concerns nirvana and its attainment. Even though Buddhists commonly insist that knowledge of the dharma is in principle accessible to anyone, still they regard Gautama's discovery and teaching of the dharma as unique in this era.

Consider how the conversation might proceed at this point. If my Buddhist friend should caution me that I will never attain nirvana by following the course of life laid out for me by the Christian community, I do not feel anxious about this. I have not been persuaded that seeking nirvana is what I should be doing. If I did begin to be persuaded of this, then I should undertake to discover the path and try to make my way along it. I would, in other words, have begun to be a follower of the Buddha. I might even then join a Buddhist community or at least become an inquirer. Some Christians I know have done this very thing. But if I continue to be convinced that it is salvation that I should be seeking and that Christ is the unique mediator of this salvation, then I would continue on the Christian path.

One thing to notice about this hypothetical conversation between me and my Buddhist friend is that I have not felt affronted by her warning that I shall not attain nirvana unless I follow the Excellent Eightfold Path taught uniquely by the Buddha. On the contrary, my initial reaction is that what she has said to me makes perfect sense. If the Excellent Eightfold Path is the way to nirvana and if I do not choose to pursue this path, then it follows that I may not reach nirvana. But, since I have as yet no desire to attain and enjoy nirvana, I am not offended by this reasoning. I have not been persuaded that nirvana is what I should be seeking.

Without trying to field a definition of religion — something that has proven notoriously difficult to do — we could say that the Christian community and the Buddhist community (with their various subcommunities) seem to have some conception of an ultimate aim of life and have developed a pattern of life geared toward attaining it. Other major religious communities share this tendency as well. What is ultimate, whether it be a transcendent agent or an as-yet unrealized state of being, invades life at every moment and summons the community's members to order and shape their lives in view of this aim. The world's religious communities differ in their descriptions of the aims that are ultimate in this sense (e.g., the extinction of the self or communion with the Triune God) as well as in their provision for the cultivation of patterns of life ordered to the attainment and enjoyment of such aims (e.g., the dharma or the gospel). But they seem to agree in espousing and commending comprehensive aims of life and in striving to shape the lives of their members with a view to those aims.

We can now state a preliminary result of the consideration of the hypothetical conversation between me and my Buddhist friend. If the assertion "The Buddha is the unique revealer of the dharma" is not offensive to me, then why should the assertion "Jesus Christ is the unique mediator of salvation" be offensive to Buddhists or, for that matter, to Muslims, Vedantists, or Jews? A rabbi once said to me, revealingly, "Jesus Christ is the answer to a question I have never asked." This remark suggests that we might be on the right track in our reflections. Salvation in the Christian sense, it implies, is not what the rabbi is seeking. Asking the question to which Jesus Christ is the answer commits oneself to an inquiry (logically speaking) that may lead to the adoption of a Christian way of life. At least in part, this will mean that what Christians aim for, as expressed by the umbrella term salvation, has begun to look appealing or even ultimately important. One might conclude: This is what I should be aiming for in my life. But what would this be?

When Christians try to answer this question, we find ourselves becoming quite specific. When we try to say what comprises salvation, we find ourselves talking about the Triune God; the incarnation, passion, death, and resurrection of Jesus Christ; grace, sin, and justification; transfiguration and divinization; faith, hope, and charity; the commandments and the moral virtues; and many other characteristically Christian things as well. We should not be surprised if, in trying to answer a cognate question, a member of another religious community, say a Buddhist, should also become very specific about nirvana and all that bears on its attainment. We should not be surprised, furthermore, if the descriptions of salvation and nirvana do not coincide. But, for the moment, let us continue the experiment by sketching some of the things that a Christian description of salvation might have to include.

Allowing for variations across its various subcommunities, we can understand the ecumenical Christian community to teach that the ultimate aim of life is a communion of life — a communion of life with the Father, through the Son, and in the Holy Spirit. According to ecumenical Christian faith, this is a truth proclaimed by Christ and a destiny made possible for us by his passion, death, and resurrection. This is what Christians mean by salvation: the term embraces both the goal of ultimate communion and the empowerment to attain and enjoy it.

Human beings are called to nothing less than communion with the Father, Son, and Holy Spirit and with one another in them. Indeed, Christianity affirms that the Triune God could not bring about a more intimate union with created persons than that which has already been initiated in baptism and will be fulfilled for us in Christ. Ultimate communion involves nothing less than becoming part of the trinitarian family. The principle and agent of this communion for us is Christ. Just as Christ is Son by nature — member of the divine family of the Trinity in virtue of his being the Son of the Father — so human persons are to be sons and daughters by adoption. Our fellowship with Christ and with each other in him brings us into the divine trinitarian family.

But if we are destined to enjoy this ultimate communion, then we must change. We must become fit for it. Interpersonal communion is "natural" to the uncreated persons within God; for created persons, who are also sinners, such communion is possible only through justification and grace. Through the redeeming grace of Christ and, specifically, through the transformation that this grace makes possible, we are rendered "fit" participants in the communion of the Father, Son, and Holy Spirit. Our transformation will be a conformation: the more we become like Christ, the more surely do we discover our true selves, the unique persons created by the Triune God to share in the divine life and to enjoy the personal life of the Trinity. As Catholics pray in one of the Sunday prefaces, "Father... You sent him as one like ourselves, though free from sin, that you might see and love in us what you see and love in him."

However, this conformation does not amount to a mere conformity. The conformation to Christ that is the principle of our transformation is not a mere cloning but the realization of our distinctive and unique personal identities. This must be so, for otherwise the communion to which this transformation is directed could not be consummated. The image of God in us consists precisely in the spiritual capacities for knowing and loving that make interpersonal communion possible. But authentic interpersonal communion presupposes the full realization of the individual persons who enter into it. Thus, if Christ is to be the principle and pattern of our transformation, in being conformed to him we must each discover and realize our own unique identities as persons and be healed of the sinful dispositions that obstruct the flourishing of our true selves.

This is the force of the astonishing saying of Christ that if any want to be his disciple, they must deny themselves and take up their cross and follow him. For those who want to save their life will lose it, and those who lose their life for Christ's sake will find it (see Matt. 16:24–26). None of us, whether as teachers, parents, or pastors — no matter how inflated our conceptions of ourselves or how confident our sense of our abilities — would ever dare to say to those in our charge that they will find their true selves by imitating us. In effect, Christ asserts that an indefinite number of human persons will find their distinctive identities by being conformed to him. A moment's reflection shows us that only the Son of God could make such an assertion. No mere human could do so. Only the inexhaustibly rich, perfect image of God who is the person of the Son in a human nature could constitute the principle and pattern for the transformation and fulfillment of every human person who has ever lived.

When Christians affirm that Jesus Christ is the unique mediator of salvation, something like the above can stand as a summary of what they mean. Leave aside for a moment the question whether such a description includes or excludes persons who are not Christians. What we need to consider first, as we continue to reflect on my hypothetical conversation with a Buddhist friend, is whether such a description of what Christians mean by salvation is offensive to persons who are not Christians — Buddhists, for example. Informed of what a Christian means by salvation, would there be reason for a Buddhist to feel excluded by the assertion that Jesus Christ is the unique mediator of salvation?

We have seen that salvation has a specific content for Christians: it entails an interpersonal communion, made possible by Christ, between human persons and the Father, Son, and Holy Spirit. At least at first sight, this seems to be something very different from what Buddhists can be supposed to be seeking when they follow the Excellent Eightfold Path that leads them on the way to realizing enlightenment and the extinction of self in nirvana. At least on the face of things, what Buddhists mean by nirvana and what Christians mean by salvation do not seem to coincide. This does not mean that they are opposed; it remains to be seen whether seeking salvation and seeking nirvana are complementary to each other or related in some as-yet unspecified manner. However, it seems clear that interpersonal communion is a very different thing from the extinction of the self entailed in nirvana. Many forms of Buddhism are concerned to cultivate dispositions that increasingly unmask the illusoriness of personal identity. As noted above, however, Christians understand personal identity to be of permanent, indeed eternal, significance because eternity centrally involves interpersonal communion.

Let us return to my hypothetical conversation with my Buddhist friend. We left the conversation at the point where she cautioned me that I would not reach nirvana unless I followed the Excellent Eightfold Path. But this warning was not disturbing to me, for I do not want to attain nirvana. Suppose that when the conversation resumes, I offer a description of what Christians mean by salvation, a description not unlike the one presented above. Would we be surprised to find that my Buddhist friend wants no part of this? It is difficult for us to understand and accept that what we regard as most important — more so than anything else, absolutely speaking — other religious people challenge or repudiate. Buddhist communities in all their variety possess highly ramified teachings about the true aim of life and about the means to attain it. These teachings do not, at least on the surface, coincide with what Christians teach about these matters. Buddhists do not want ultimate communion; they do not seek it, and insofar as they think about it, they may regard us as misguided for wanting and seeking it. For by wanting and seeking ultimate communion, we remain, from a Buddhist point of view, incorrigibly attached to the very conceptions of personal identity that constitute the chief obstacle on the way to nirvana.

Gautama the Buddha is the authority on these matters. His followers believe that he discovered and taught the dharma and through it attained enlightenment. His role in revealing the dharma to others is regarded by most of his followers as something original, at least in the present epoch. Hence, while it makes good sense for Buddhists to affirm that the Buddha is the unique revealer of the dharma, it makes little sense for them to be offended when Christians describe Jesus Christ as the unique mediator of salvation. Buddhists regard Christian beliefs about this as misguided and perhaps only partially true, but they will not be anxious or offended by such a Christian affirmation. They are not interested in seeking and attaining salvation as Christians understand it.

To be sure, some people — pluralists in particular — want to define salvation so broadly that it includes both what Christians mean by it and what Buddhists mean by nirvana. On this account of things, my hypothetical encounter with a Buddhist friend would not present either of us with a choice between seeking nirvana and seeking salvation. Some would say that to think that there is a serious choice here is, religiously speaking, overly literalistic and even simpleminded. Indeed, pluralists contend that precisely at this juncture is the superiority of pluralist theology of religions displayed. Pluralists argue that all religious communities advance their members toward specific aims — communion or enlightenment, as the case may be — that are surpassed or transcended by a more ultimate, but indescribable, aim. All religious communities seek this yet more ultimate aim with varying degrees of clarity and success. Not only is this conception closer to the truth of the matter; it also provides the basis for the sympathetic understanding, fruitful dialogue, and mutual respect that are desperately needed today.

In fact, however, this basic premise of pluralist theology of religions will not stand up under close scrutiny. Even if religious communities were prepared to accept some such description of what they are about, it still remains true that they espouse and commend specific aims that differ from one another. Furthermore, these specific aims call forth distinctive patterns of life in each of the major religious traditions and in local traditions as well. Certain kinds of life are understood to foster the enjoyment of certain kinds of ends of life, and others to obstruct this enjoyment. This seems to be an ineradicable feature of the characteristic discourse and ethos of most religious communities. Individual lives come to be shaped by the ultimate aims that are sought. So even if the true aim of life were one that transcended the particular aims of all religious traditions, no one could seek it. No one could undertake to order life in such a way as to attain and enjoy an ultimate aim of life of which no description could be given. But this goes directly against the grain of characteristic religious affirmation and conviction.

Religious people, by and large, believe themselves to be in possession of understandings, incomplete though they may be, of what is ultimately important in life and how to orient life in its direction. Significant disagreements obtain among the major and local religious traditions about these matters. Pluralist theology of religions does not so much explain these disagreements as explain them away. In this way, pluralism seems to offer a massive redescription, rather than an interpretation, of religious beliefs and practices and of the arresting differences among them.

The following statements are not problematic in the way that many people seem to think: Jesus Christ is the unique mediator of salvation, and the Buddha is the unique revealer of the dharma. Were representatives of Christian or Buddhist communities to retreat from advancing such claims, it is not clear what they would have to offer to the world. There would be no compelling, or even interesting, reasons to persevere in membership in these communities, or indeed to seek it.

The great challenge facing present-day Christian theology of religions and interreligious conversation is to avoid minimizing the distinctive features of the major religious traditions through a well-intentioned universalism. Christian confidence in the universal scope of salvation rests on convictions about the historical career and perduring agency of Jesus Christ. Only if his identity is affirmed in its fullness — in accord with the Holy Scripture, the great councils, and the church's liturgy — as the Son of God who became man and died for us can the hope of Christians for themselves and for others be sustained. "For in him all the fulness of God was pleased to dwell, and through him to reconcile to himself all things, whether on earth or in heaven, making peace by the blood of his cross" (Col. 1:19–20).

If the salvation that the Triune God wills for the entire human race entails ultimate communion with the three persons, then the creaturely and sinful obstacles to this communion must be overcome. It has never been claimed that anyone but Jesus Christ could overcome these obstacles. Through him we are both healed and raised to an adoptive participation in the life of the Trinity. The obstacles to this participation are either overcome or not. If they are not overcome, then Christians have nothing for which to hope, for themselves or for others. In that case, they will hawk an empty universalism on the highways of the world. When Christians abandon the proclamation of Christ's unique mediatorship, they have no other mediatorship with which to replace it.

How persons who are not now explicit believers in Christ can actually come to share in the salvation he alone makes possible is a large topic that I have not addressed here. But if Christians no longer confess Christ's unique mediatorship in making ultimate communion a real possibility for created persons, then the problem of how non-Christians can share in it is not resolved: it simply evaporates. True Christian universalism depends on the affirmation of the nonexclusive particularity of salvation in Jesus Christ. The particularism of God's execution of the plan of salvation does not cancel out the universalism of this plan.

So it turns out that both our concern to be respectful to other religions and their adherents and our concern to do justice to God's universal salvific will depend crucially on our being able to give a resoundingly affirmative answer to the question we have considered here: Is Jesus Christ the unique mediator of salvation? We need to keep together both parts of the passage from 1 Timothy with which we began: "God our Savior ... desires all men to be saved and to come to the knowledge of the truth. For there is one God, and there is one mediator between God and men, the man Christ Jesus, who gave himself as a ransom for all" (1 Tim. 2:3–5).

For Further Reading

D'Costa, Gavin. *Theology and Religious Pluralism.* Oxford: Blackwell, 1986. Helpful survey of the literature, with the adoption of a broadly inclusivist position dependent on Karl Rahner.

D'Costa, Gavin, ed. *Christian Uniqueness Reconsidered.* Maryknoll, N.Y.: Orbis, 1990. Essays in response to the pluralist theologies of religion in Hick and Knitters, eds., *The Myth of Christian Uniqueness.*

Di Noia, J. A. *The Diversity of Religions: A Christian Perspective.* Washington, D.C.: Catholic University of America Press, 1992. Consideration of the ends non-Christian religions claim for themselves, and a Christian evaluation thereof.

Griffiths, Paul, ed. *Christianity through Non-Christian Eyes.* Maryknoll, N.Y.: Orbis, 1990. Helpful anthology of non-Christian views of Christianity.

Heim, S. Mark. *Salvations: Truth and Difference in Religion.* Maryknoll, N.Y.: Orbis, 1995. Critique of pluralist theologies and argument for different salvations through different religions.

Hick, John, and Paul Knitter, eds. *The Myth of Christian Uniqueness.* Maryknoll, N.Y.: Orbis, 1987. Anthology of pluralist theologies of religion.

Sullivan, Francis A. *Salvation outside the Church?* New York: Paulist, 1995. Historical survey of magisterial and theological teaching.

Vatican Council II. "Declaration on the Relation of the Church to Non-Christian Religions" in *Vatican Council II: The Conciliar and Post Conciliar Documents,* Austin Flannery, gen. ed. Wilmington, Del.: Scholarly Resources, 1975, pp. 738–42. Magisterial document foundational for current debate and practice.

5

ARE THERE ANGELS?

Bruce D. Marshall

Angels Abounding

Should you ever be curious whether the person you are talking to in the checkout line at the grocery store is a theologian, there is probably no more effective way to find out than to ask that person whether she or he believes in angels. Among the guild of professional theologians in America today, serious talk about angels is roughly as common as serious talk about Santa Claus or the tooth fairy. If theologians bring the subject up at all, it is ordinarily not to debate whether or not angels actually exist, but to lament the prevalence of superstition among the rest of the population. We theologians, indeed, tend to think that one of the chief tasks in our job description is to rescue other people from their own credulity. Some of my colleagues have shown the film *The Rapture* in class, but not without worrying that its vivid depiction of the apocalypse — avenging angels and all — might lead impressionable undergraduates to believe that the world could actually come to an end in the manner the Book of Revelation describes.

When it comes to angels, we clearly have our work cut out for us. If theologians find it difficult to take angels seriously, great numbers of Americans do not. The last decade has witnessed an explosion of interest in angels, not just among more traditionally minded Christians, from whom angels have always received a certain degree of attention, but in the population at large. There are angel movies, angel TV specials, a highly rated weekly family drama about angels, and — perhaps most disheartening of all, if your job description calls for vigilance about credulity — a deluge of angel books. It is the literate, book-reading public that has taken to angels. There are, of course, lots of books on Santa Claus as well, but these are books that adults read to their children; the angel books they are reading for themselves. A lot of adults clearly believe in angels, or wish they could. Is this a sad example of the kind of credulity to which even educated people are unhappily subject, or is there some reasonable possibility that belief in angels could be true?

In order to decide whether something exists, we have to have some idea of what we are looking for. If a coelacanth is a deep-sea fish so primitive that it provides a living link with the age of the dinosaurs, then it seems that coelacanths do exist (or at least they did in the middle of this century, though none has been found recently). If a coelacanth is a winged species of horse, one of whose number is named Pegasus, then it seems that coelacanths do not exist. So it is with angels. Whether we can reasonably suppose that angels exist depends on what we are talking about — what we have in mind — when we speak of angels.

Although theologians today (with some important exceptions) generally have little interest in angels, it was not always so. For much of Christian history, angels were a standard topic of theological discussion, and the Christian tradition has developed a rich and complex view of angels and their work in the world. The tradition's interest in angels chiefly stems, of course, from the Bible, which has something to say about angels — but is also, as we shall see, sometimes notably silent about them. In order to get at the question of whether there are angels, we will first have to formulate a reasonably clear idea of what it is we are looking for — of what we are talking about when we speak of *angels*. We will do that by examining some beliefs about angels currently afoot in the popular media in light of what the Bible and the Christian tradition have to say about angels. The effect will be to generate a distinctively Christian notion of what an angel is, or would be. We can then think about deciding whether there are such things.

The Idea of All Angels

As they tend to be depicted in the current wave of movies and books, angels have a lot in common with humans, though they also have some wonderful powers that we lack. Media angels often look, walk, and talk like human beings. Indeed only the receptive eye can distinguish them from ordinary humans; the plot of many angel stories turns on the moment when a stubborn person, after repeated visitations by what just seem like very friendly and helpful people, realizes she or he has been entertaining angels unawares. Even when angels come on the scene in a supernatural or uncanny way — flapping their wings, hovering in midair, or surrounded by fuzzy light — they usually have manifestly human features. Their appearance is meant to be comforting and reassuring, not only because they can do things for us that are, at least for the moment, beyond our powers (throw a blinding fastball, start our snowbound car on a lonely road, or find a set of keys), but because these powers emanate from creatures whose kindness, forgiveness, and concern for us exceeds that which we expect to receive from other human beings. The only barrier to our enjoyment of the comfort the angels are here to provide is our own lack of receptivity — our failure to believe in them.

Just as popular angelology tends to depict angels as superhumans — a lot like us at our best, only better — it also tends to depict humans as lesser angels or, perhaps more precisely, potential angels. According to this view, what happens to us when we die is that we become angels, and angels are dead human beings. Thus the "angels in the outfield," of the recent movie of that title, are former humans, and one of the human characters, we are told near the end of the movie, is about to join them. The suggestion is generally made, though, that becoming an angel is conditional. We have to show some angelic kindness and forbearance in this life, and perhaps we even need to change someone else's life the way angels do, in order to enjoy an angelic existence later on. We have to display some of the moral qualities of angels, in other words, in order to have the fun that goes with possessing superhuman powers.

One of the striking aspects of the way the Bible talks about angels is that though they appear quite often, they are rarely described. When the angel Gabriel appears to Mary of Nazareth and announces to her that she is full of grace and the favor of God and will be the mother of God's Son (Luke 1:26–38) — certainly as important an angelic encounter as takes place in the Bible, and one of the very few times a biblical angel has a name — Luke makes no comment about what Gabriel looks like. Mary is clearly troubled by the angel's greeting; she is, after all, a virgin. What gets her attention, however, is not that she has seen an angel. The issue in Luke's narrative is not whether Mary believes in angels, and there is no suggestion that believing in angels is, by itself, of any special significance or value. The story turns on whether Mary believes what the angel *said*, on whether she trusts God enough to accept the astonishing announcement God makes to her by way of the angel: "She was much perplexed by his words, and pondered what sort of greeting this might be.... And blessed is she who believed that there would be a fulfillment of what was spoken to her by the Lord" (Luke 1:29, 45). In Matthew's account of Jesus' birth Joseph, rather than Mary, receives the angelic visits (Matt. 1:20; 2:13), but here too the angel's features — if indeed the angel has any — are not described.

In a few biblical passages we do, to be sure, get a vivid depiction of angels. But these descriptions of angelic physical features emphasize how different angels are from human beings, rather than what we and they have in common. Isaiah sees seraphs with six wings hovering over God's throne in the inner sanctuary of the Jerusalem temple (Isa. 6:2). In Ezekiel's elaborate vision of the heavenly court, he sees "something like four living creatures" that appeared to be "of human form" (Ezek. 1:5). But we should not be misled by this: though these "living creatures" have the basic shape ("form") of human beings, they are anything but human. Each has four hands, four wings, and, most startling of all, four faces; one of these is human, but the others have the features of a lion, an ox, and an eagle (Ezek. 1:6–11). In the New Testament the one description of the features of angels is clearly a variant on Ezekiel's vision. Seeing four living creatures around the heavenly throne of God, the author of Revelation sharpens the contrast between these beings and us by noting that they are "full of eyes in front and behind... all around and inside" (Rev. 4:6, 8). Not surprisingly,

these visions of angels are not so much comforting to their re-
cipients as astounding and even terrifying. "Woe is me!" cries
Isaiah, "for I am lost" (Isa. 6:5); Ezekiel falls on his face, unable
to rise (Ezek. 1:28). And while angels bring messages of comfort
to persecuted churches (at least to some of them) in Revelation
2–3, it is also angels who blow the trumpets of apocalyptic destruction in Revelation 8–9 and who pour out the bowls of
God's wrath in Revelation 16.

The Christian theological tradition has sharpened the biblical contrast between angels and human beings by arguing that
angels do not have bodies at all. In this tradition angels are
pure spirits, pure minds that can think and act, but do not
need bodies to do so (even though they sometimes appear in
bodily form). Human beings by contrast are embodied spirits,
creatures who can think and act (like the angels and ultimately,
of course, like God), but who require bodies in order to exist
at all.

Although it is surely fair to observe that the long theological tradition of speculation about the angels as pure spiritual
intelligences goes beyond anything the Bible says about angels, the tradition is nonetheless deeply biblical in its insistence
that humans and angels should not be confused with one another. Angels are a different kind of thing from humans, just
as we humans are a different kind of thing from antelopes or
aphids. This is the way God wants it; he makes a universe
at once richly diverse and suitably ordered, filled with countless different kinds of things, but where everything comes forth
"according to its kind" (as Gen. 1 has it). Just as God's creation would be poorer — less beautiful — without antelopes
and aphids, so it would be poorer without angels. But just as
human beings are not created by God to become antelopes or
aphids, to exist according to some other kind, so we are not
created to become angels. According to the Christian theological tradition, human beings are not lesser angels or angels in
training — angel wanna-bes. We are now what we will always
be: embodied spirits, human beings.

This tradition is also surely biblical in locating the heart of
the divinely willed difference between us and the angels in the
fact that we have bodies. Although the angels sometimes appear

in bodily form, these incidents are clearly atypical; in the ordinary run of things, biblical angels are invisible. That human beings are not invisible, and so cannot over the long run hide from one another, is no accident but goes with having a body. In our essential bodiliness, we human beings are like the other animals, the plants, and indeed the dirt from which (so Gen. 2:7 relates) we were made. We are the sort of thing that takes up space and time; although we have thought and action in common with the angels, we also have something in common with the most humble parts of God's creation: with the worms and with the mud and earth in which they dwell.

As God did not make us angelic, but embodied, so the destiny he wills for us we can only attain in our bodies. In the New Testament the destiny for which God made us is life with God and in God, an inexhaustible share in the infinity of God's own life. We are to become, as 2 Peter 1:4 has it, "participants of the divine nature." It seems clear that such an unfathomable degree of intimacy with God can be reached only if our death is overcome. Now it is just on account of having bodies that we die. So if our death is to be overcome, if our very selves are to get beyond death, then our bodies must rise from the dead. "For this perishable body must put on imperishability," the apostle Paul proclaims, "and this mortal body must put on immortality. When this perishable body puts on imperishability, and this mortal body puts on immortality, then the saying that is written will be fulfilled: 'Death has been swallowed up in victory' " (1 Cor. 15:53–54). If our bodies were finally dispensable, if our selves could get along without them, then we could get beyond death and get to God by leaving our bodies behind. We would then, perhaps, be something like angels. But if, as the New Testament apparently claims, our selves cannot get beyond death except by having God raise our bodies to life, then our bodies forever belong to who we are. For we human beings to be deprived of our bodies would be for us, not to become angels, but to perish.

A passage like Luke 20:35–36 ("In the resurrection from the dead...they cannot die anymore, because they are like angels and are children of God, being children of the resurrection"; cf. Matt. 22:30; Mark 12:25) should not cause any confusion on this score. The point is not that human beings can attain their destiny without their bodies (what rises, after all, is precisely what was dead, and that is, at the very least, the body). It is not in this respect that the risen dead are "like angels"; rather the risen differ from us in that they "cannot die anymore," since in the resurrection they attain their destiny as "children of God," forever to enjoy the inconceivable intimacy and friendship with God for which God made us all. The theological tradition has consistently shared this biblical insistence that the attainment of our destiny requires that we humans rise from the dead and so has insisted that the body is indispensable for genuinely human life, even when (as often) the tradition has maintained that the human soul is immortal. Even if the soul is immortal, its aim is not to get out of the body but to get back in it; the separated soul cannot fully attain the life for which God made it until, in the end, it is reunited with the body God gave it.

That we human beings can never become angels might seem a depressing and frustrating thought; from the vantage point of some current quests for "angel consciousness," this would consign us forever to an inferior form of existence. Interestingly, the Christian theological tradition has long held that we have no need to envy the angels. Indeed from an early point in Christian history theologians regularly argued that those angels who lost the high position in which God created them fell from grace precisely because they envied *us*. Here may be found the ancient tradition that the devil, and with him the "principalities and powers" of which the New Testament (especially Paul) speaks, is a fallen angel. Gregory of Nyssa, writing in the late fourth century, describes the devil's fall: "The angel to whom the administration of the earth's affairs had been allotted found it absurd, indeed insufferable, that from the creatures which were under his authority there should arise a being made in the image and likeness of God's own transcendent beauty" — a reference to Genesis 1:26–27, where it is specifically humans, and not angels, who are created to resemble God in a special way. This means that human beings, even though they have bodies and so lack powers that the angels possess, are in the natural order of things more like, and so closer to, God than the angels; accord-

ing to this ancient tradition, the angels fell because they lacked
the humility to accept the superiority, the greater God-likeness,
of creatures less powerful than they.

A parallel tradition argues that some of the angels fell because they were too proud to accept the unique and supreme
intimacy God willed to have, not with them, but with us. For
God did not become one of them, but became one of us: "it
is clear that he did not take angels to himself, but rather the
seed of Abraham" (Heb. 2:16). God has become incarnate; in
Jesus Christ he has made our flesh and blood, our body and
our death, his own. In Jesus' resurrection and ascension, our
human flesh and blood have been exalted to "the right hand of
the Majesty on high" so that Jesus of Nazareth, a human being, has "become as much superior to angels as the name he
has inherited is more excellent than theirs" (Heb. 1:3–4). This
mystery of God's descent to us in Christ, and our ascent to God
in him, the gospel reveals to us; believers in the gospel need not
envy the angels their place since into the mystery of which the
gospel speaks "angels long to look" (1 Pet. 1:12). In the Christian tradition it seems that having a human body, which forever
bars us from being angels, is not such a bad thing; for our sake,
God now and forever has one too.

What Angels Do

We have so far spoken mainly about what angels *are*, or are
thought to be. We cannot take up the question whether angels
actually exist without also considering what angels *do*, or are
thought to do.

According to today's popular angelology, as I have already
suggested, what angels mainly do is provide extraordinary support and reassurance to ordinary people. They rescue stranded
motorists; throw, lift, or just nudge distracted pedestrians from
the path of speeding automobiles; help lost travelers get on the
right train; and fill distressed and despondent people with a
sense of warmth and well-being. They ease our bafflement and
incompetence at daily life in an industrial and technological age,
and they ease the loneliness and isolation all too common in
modern society. As one contemporary angel writer puts it, the

angels "play with us. They look after us. They heal us, comfort us with invisible warm hands, and always they try to give us what we want." While not all contemporary angelologists would perhaps put the point so baldly, the basic idea of much popular angel literature does seem to be that the mission of the angels is to fulfill our individual wants and needs as we perceive them. The angels are an ever-present resource into which we can tap for emotional health, personal improvement, and perhaps even emergency rescue. Perhaps much of the current reliance on angels stems from this sense that they can meet quite common daily needs more readily and reliably than our fellow humans or social institutions, if only we can open our hearts and minds enough to believe in them.

That each human being has an angel who cares for him or her — a guardian angel — is in fact a well-established Christian idea, amply supported by the theologians of the ancient church. At least one story in the New Testament seems to suggest this idea, when Peter, freed from prison by an angel, is himself mistaken for "his angel" by the disciples (Acts 12:15; cf. also Matt. 18:10). Even this episode, however, only serves to underline the basic character of angelic action in the Bible. In contrast to today's media angels, biblical angels chiefly act, not for the sake of the individuals to whom they come, but always for a larger purpose. Correlatively, biblical angels do not so much comfort as call to action; they bring not relief but exertion. Peter is freed from prison by an angel, not because he found being in chains a depressing experience (though it would be fair to assume that he did), but in order that he might continue preaching the gospel, even at the cost of his life. Isaiah and Ezekiel get to see angels, not in order to reassure them that life has a spiritual dimension or to help them cope with the perplexities of daily life, but in order to equip them for the difficult prophetic work that lies ahead. An angel announces to Mary that she is blessed, not in order to give her what she already wants, but to help her want what only someone full of grace could possibly desire: to bear the crucified Redeemer of the world in her womb.

The larger purpose for which angels act in the Bible is that embodied with particular clarity in Gabriel's mission to Mary:

the salvation of the world. "Are not all angels," asks the author of the Letter to the Hebrews, "spirits in the divine service,
sent to serve for the sake of those who are to inherit salvation?" (Heb. 1:14). The angels are not here to serve us — to
give us what we think we want — but to serve God and God's
overarching purpose of salvation in human life and history. Biblical angels point us, not to themselves, but to God and the still
ongoing story of God's own saving action and presence in the
world. The Bible displays no interest in angels for their own
sake (as we have seen, it rarely even describes them). We know
about the angels at all only from the role they play in the story
of salvation that embraces the history of Israel, Jesus Christ,
and the church and that will end only with Christ's return in
glory. In this story the angels have a role as servants; their place
in the unfolding drama is genuine, but subordinate. The chief
actors are God and human beings.

The heart of the drama of salvation, so Christians believe, is
Jesus' life, death, and resurrection. Here the role of the angels
in God's redemptive enterprise comes most clearly into focus.
An angel announces the Redeemer soon to be and waits upon
Mary's assent that he be born at all. Angels declare Jesus' birth
to the world (Luke 2:13–14) and see to the survival of the
threatened infant Redeemer (Matt. 2:13). Angels care for him
after he has resisted the devil's temptations (Matt. 4:11; Mark
1:13). Jesus forgoes the help of angelic legions in obedience to
the Father's will that he die by crucifixion (Matt. 26:53–54).
The angels accept this limitation on their action; they will do
only what they are sent to do by the Father and the Son. But
the Son is not abandoned in the suffering that his obedience entails; the Father, so Luke relates, consoles Jesus by sending an
angel to strengthen him in his resolve to obey the Father's will
(Luke 22:43).

Above all, biblical angels are witnesses and messengers of the
resurrection. In all the Gospels it is angels who first proclaim
to human beings the good news of Jesus' rising. They guard the
now-empty tomb (keep watch, as it were, over the now-open
gates of death; cf. John 20:12–13) and initially announce the
resurrection to the first visitors at the tomb (cf. Matt. 28:2–7),
or (as Mark 16:7 and Luke 24:4–9 stress) announce the fulfill-

ment of Jesus' own promise that he would rise from the dead. Yet as these accounts make clear, it is only by seeing and touching Jesus' risen flesh that human beings, including those who hear the angels' proclamation, actually come to believe in his resurrection for the first time. And the task of proclaiming the gospel of salvation to the world is entrusted not to angels but to human beings, though not without ongoing angelic support and guidance (not least, e.g., in the decision to offer the gospel to Gentiles as well as to Jews; cf. Acts 10:3ff.).

Angels, then, serve God's saving purpose in history by doing what God commands; apart from this role in the story of salvation, the Bible seems to have no interest in them. God's saving purpose, we have observed, is to give humans an inconceivably intimate share in his own life, to establish forever in Jesus Christ what the Christian tradition has long called *friendship* between himself and us. The angels serve this purpose, not by directing us toward themselves, but by directing us toward God in the crucified and risen Jesus Christ. As the biblical role ascribed to the angels makes clear, we finally find the friendship and fulfillment for which we all long, not in intimacy with the angels themselves, but with God; "our heart," as Saint Augustine long ago called out to God alone in prayer, "is restless until it rests in you."

Biblical angels do serve God, however, not simply by acting in time to direct humans to God, but by worshiping God themselves. Isaiah and Ezekiel do not simply see angels; they see angels wholly devoted to the praise of God. The Christian community, gathered by the Spirit around the Word and sacrament of the risen Jesus and awaiting his return in glory, already shares in the heavenly liturgy of the angels and the saints: "you have come to Mount Zion and to the city of the living God, the heavenly Jerusalem, and to innumerable angels in festal gathering, and to the assembly of the firstborn who are enrolled in heaven" (Heb. 12:22–23; cf. the vivid depictions of the heavenly liturgy in Rev. 4–5; 7:9–8:5; 11:15–18; 15:2–8; 19:1–8). That in both time and eternity we do not worship or pray to the angels, but join them in the worship of God, indicates with particular clarity that our interest in the angels, like their interest in us, is not for their own sake but for God's sake. When

the author of Revelation falls down to worship the angel who
has let him see the heavenly Jerusalem, the angel bids John to
stand: "You must not do that! I am a fellow servant," the angel
insists, "with you and your comrades who hold the testimony
of Jesus. Worship God!" (Rev. 19:10; cf. 22:9).

So Are There Angels?

As we observed at the outset, many theologians today would
continue to take the view that the German Protestant theologian Rudolf Bultmann articulated over a generation ago: "The
belief in spirits and demons has been superseded as a result of
our knowledge of the powers and laws of nature." Such robust confidence in the omnicompetence of modern science will
strike many people (including many scientists) today as a bit
quaint. We now tend to suppose, more than in Bultmann's day,
that scientific knowledge has limits as well as wondrous accomplishments, and we are now used to the idea that good
science involves imagination and speculation as well as observation and calculation. Ruling out belief in the existence of angels
as unscientific today seems more rash than it once did.

But do we have any good reason to believe that angels actually exist? It is one thing to suggest that even the best science
has its limits and quite another to populate the world beyond
the borders of science with exotic beings, angelic or otherwise.
The current passion for angels may well be bound up with a
longing to believe that there is more wonder and enchantment
to human life than science can tell us about, or than the commercial amusements to which we turn at the end of our long,
technologically overloaded workday can provide. But wishing
doesn't make it so. The question remains whether we have any
more reason to believe in angels than in Santa Claus or the
tooth fairy.

Popular angelology handles this question by appealing to the
personal experience of those who have had encounters with
angels. This is surely why most of the space in today's angel
books is taken up with stories, generally in the first person,
of angel experiences. Although this material is often of the
I-turned-around-to-thank-the-stranger-who-helped-me-onto-

the-train-and-he-had-vanished variety, it would be unfair to dismiss all of it as the product of mere credulity. Sometimes perfectly responsible people do have uncanny experiences in everyday life that defy ordinary sorts of explanation. But one can grant that point and still wonder whether there is any good reason to chalk up these experiences to angelic intervention, rather than to some other cause, known or unknown. Moreover, we are all familiar with finding that moving or unsettling experiences, not least when they respond to some deeply felt need, have deceived us: we were sure it was so, but we were wrong. ("At last the girl at the desk next to mine has smiled at me. She must really, though secretly, like me.")

The very *idea* of angels that prevails in current popular accounts makes it difficult to respond to such doubts about whether angels really exist. According to this idea, what angels are for is chiefly to give us warm and comforting experiences. These experiences, moreover, are supposed to be for *me;* my angel helps and comforts me because she or he is looking out specifically for my welfare. Since such experiences sometimes lead us astray ("She smiled at me, but . . . "), yet are pretty much the only basis popular accounts give us for believing in angels, there seems no way to resolve doubts about the reality of this sort of angel. And since these angels seem concerned almost exclusively with the private well-being of individuals, if I have not had a personal encounter with one, I have no reason to believe in this sort of angel at all — for all I know, my angel is asleep, or there aren't enough angels to go around.

The angels of which the Bible and the Christian tradition speak are of a different sort, and the grounds we have for believing in them are, I think, straightforward. These angels are there, not primarily to serve individual needs, but to serve God and God's purpose of salvation. We know about what they do and what they are only from the secondary but seemingly inextricable role they play in the ongoing story of God's saving work in the world. Whether we have reason to believe in this sort of angel does not depend, therefore, on whether we have had a personal encounter with one. Believing in biblical angels depends, rather, on believing that the biblical story of salvation, in which alone these angels have a place, is true.

The story of salvation, as also of the angels' mission, turns on the story of Jesus, above all on the story of Jesus' resurrection. In this story the angels have a role that belongs to them alone; above all they are, as I have suggested, the first creaturely witnesses to Jesus' resurrection. The question of whether there are angels — this kind of angel — seems to come down, therefore, to the question of whether the story of Jesus is true. If Jesus is risen from the dead or, more precisely, if the belief that Jesus is risen from the dead is true, then we have good reason to believe in angels. That is, the angels are in their own distinctive way messengers of the good news of Jesus' resurrection; so if the story that culminates in this good news is true, it is surely plausible also to believe in those creaturely witnesses who first announce it (though it is perhaps debatable whether the role of the angels is so deeply a part of the story of Jesus' rising that believing this story to be true *requires* us to believe in angels). Should on the contrary the belief that Jesus is risen be false, then there is no Good News, and so no need of messengers, angelic or otherwise, to proclaim it. If Jesus is not risen, then we have little reason to believe that there are angels; nor would it matter much if there were.

For Further Reading

Augustine. *The City of God.* Trans. Henry Bettenson. London and New York: Penguin Books, 1984. Especially Book XI. As with Calvin and Chemnitz, a classic theological account of the angels and what they do.

Balthasar, Hans Urs von. *Theo-Drama,* vol 3. Trans. Graham Harrison. San Francisco: Ignatius Press, 1992, pp. 465–501. As with Barth, a stimulating treatment of angels by an important twentieth-century theologian.

Barth, Karl. *Church Dogmatics,* vol. 3, pt. 3. Trans. G. W. Bromily and R. J. Ehrlich. Edinburgh: T. & T. Clark, 1960. §51, pp. 369–531.

Bush, Trudy. "On the Tide of the Angels." *The Christian Century,* March 1, 1995, pp. 236–38. A brief critical survey of recent angel books.

Calvin, John. *Institutes of the Christian Religion.* Trans. Ford Lewis Battles. Philadelphia: Westminster Press, 1960. Book I, chapter xiv, sections 3–12.

Chemnitz, Martin. *Loci Theologici*. Trans. J. A. O. Preus. St. Louis: Concordia, 1989. Vol. 1, locus 4, Appendix: "A Treatise on Angels."

Daniélou, Jean. *The Angels and Their Mission according to the Fathers of the Church*. Trans. David Heimann. Westminster, Md.: Christian Classics, Inc., 1976. A survey of early Christian theological views on angels.

Schlier, Heinrich. "The Angels according to the New Testament" in *The Relevance of the New Testament*. New York: Herder & Herder, 1968, pp. 172–92. A helpful biblical study.

6

WHY GO TO CHURCH?

James J. Buckley

Ways Going to Church Is Dangerous

We go to church (Paul teaches at 1 Cor. 11:26) to eat the bread and drink the cup that proclaim Christ's death until he comes in glory. What is it to do this? And why do it? I aim to answer these simple questions. But it is quite impossible to do this in any simple way because Paul's teaching is (or seems) so distant from our ordinary church-going practices. How so?

People in our culture "go to church" for an odd assortment of reasons. Some go because of familial or social pressure; some, to obey a rule of their church; and some, out of unreflective personal habit. Others go to see a boyfriend or girlfriend, to enjoy the music, to be entertained by old-time religion or modern consumer-driven extravaganzas. Still others go to be alone with the mystery of God, to pray for their addictions, to silently contemplate a God who shares their hopes as well as their anxieties. Still others go to hear the Word of God read and preached or to eat the body and drink the blood of Christ. Each of us could add still other reasons, some trivial and some profound.

What do such diverse and conflicting answers to the question of why people go to church tell us? For one thing, they tell us that the phrase *going to church* frequently masks conflicting activities. For some, going to church is a sort of cultural holiday practiced by good Americans, usually of the same race and economic class and aesthetic taste. For others, going to church is escaping from the maddening crowd for time alone, with God. For many Protestants or evangelicals, going to church is gathering for reading and preaching and singing the Scriptures. For Catholics and Orthodox Christians, going to church is assembling for communion in the body and blood of Christ. Seventh-Day Adventists go to church (on Saturday) as part of a response to God's command to keep holy the sabbath. There is, as far as I can see, no single, coherent practice of going to church in our culture—no matter what pollsters try to tell us.

But there is something else that our diverse answers to the question, Why go to church? teach us. Many people's reasons for going to church are, at their best, more complex than I have so far suggested. Few will say or admit that they go church *only* to accommodate their parents or friends or neighborhood or culture or their arbitrary tastes. But some will say that they go to church to hear and sing the Word of God or commune in Christ's body and blood *rather than* because of social pressures, because of personal habit, or because Sunday is our culture's weekly holiday. But why say "rather than" instead of "as well as"? If heeding God's word and sharing Christ's body are worth doing, why not get in the habit of doing them in a community that will pressure us to do them?

There is, I think, nothing intrinsically wrong with going to church as one of the rhythms of our ordinary (natural, some might say) lives — out of personal habit, because of familial pressures, because of good music or good company. But, if so, going to church seems to present two quite opposed but mutually supporting dangers, risks, or perils. One is the danger of merely reinforcing the rhythms of our culture's week or month or year—rhythms of race and class and taste in entertainment. Let's call this the *danger of accommodation*. The other is the danger of so isolating ourselves from those rhythms that going to church has little or no relationship to the rest of our lives — our lives as individuals and families, as workers and citizens, as disciples of Christ throughout our lives. Let's call this the *danger of isolation*.

I should emphasize that these twin dangers are not the dangers of every culture. If we lived in totalitarian lands, going to church would be a dangerous activity because it might cost us full citizenship, rewarding careers, and perhaps even our lives. There would be less danger of accommodation, and the danger of isolation, we could argue, would be worth the price. Sometimes we should embrace rather than avoid dangers. But I will restrict my concern to the circumstances of North America, where a large minority regularly go to church. I shall suggest, in what follows, that these twin dangers can only be addressed by taking seriously Paul's teaching that "as often as you eat this bread and drink this cup, you proclaim the death of the Lord until he comes in glory" (1 Cor. 11:26). Paul's teaching shows us that accommodation and isolation are abuses rather than instances of going to church. Thus, even if we resist the dangers of the abuses, going to church does not cease to be dangerous. It simply becomes dangerous in different ways than I have said so far.

Praying and Working

One lesson we can learn from considering the dangers of going to church is that your or my answer to the question, Why go to church? depends on the larger story of which going to church is a part — being a good American, Catholic or evangelical Christian, Seventh-Day Adventist, or someone else. Other chapters in this book are about aspects of that larger drama — the lives we live and beliefs we hold about who God is and who we are and who I am, about where we come from and are going, about angels and hell and other issues. Here I simply aim to suggest how some of the rhythms of praying and working reflect and embody this larger story, with all its dangers.

For example, Christians confess that God creates each and all of us in God's image out of and for the sheer love that God is. Our response to this gracious love is gratitude and thanksgiving, which we so frequently find articulated in the Jewish tradition of blessing God for all things, including meals and especially Passover celebrations. The larger story of which going to church is a part is this story of God's gracious creation of us for life with God — and our enacting our ordinary existence as praise and thanks for this extraordinary gift.

Such biblical thanks is as often prayed by "we" as "I" because our identities as God's creatures are not only individual but also social. And so we praise and thank God not only as individuals but also as a community — not only as a people dispersed throughout our neighborhoods and nation-states but also gathered together for this presiding end: praising and thanking God. Indeed, whether dispersed or gathered, we exist not simply for ourselves but for others — to give praise and thanks for those who cannot or even will not. So important is this worship that the first chapter of Genesis likens the creation of the entire world to a seven-day festival and likens God's creation to the construction of a temple for work and rest.

Of course, all this must sound dangerously idealistic, for we are hardly capable of responding with pure praise and gratitude to God. We are agents and victims of evil, who harden our hearts and the hearts of others. We scarcely know how to thank and praise each other without false flattery. How can we possibly trust our thanks and praise to God? We gripe and complain instead of calling each other to repentance — and we call each other to penitence when we should console each other. We are variously terrified by and indifferent to God's steadfast love, victims of despair as much as pride — and often not able to tell the difference.

In such dangerous circumstances, we need to remember how Israel cried out to God from their slavery, and God heard them — the liberating covenant between God and Israel embodied in their Passover feast (Exod. 2:23–25; chap. 12). And Israel could also cry out when it was the agent rather than the victim of sin — calling upon God from the depths, articulating its guilt and fear, repenting by daring to conceal its sin no more (Pss. 6; 32; 38; 51; 102; 130; 143). Our lives, gathered and dispersed, are not simply praise and thanks to God. Our ordinary lives are — that is, we are — also a petition, a beseeching, a calling upon God to create in us new hearts, to renew the face of our earth.

In and with such thanks and supplication, Christian identity is shaped in the light of the story of Jesus, who gathered men and women, calling them to an identity as disciples in a community of Jew and Greek, male and female, slave and free. The discipline of Jesus' discipleship included praying and eating with the disciples and crowds, telling them stories about the often enigmatic hosts and guests of future meals, miraculously providing the crowds with more food than they could possibly eat. But the most extraordinary gathering was in more dangerous circumstances. On the night he was betrayed, Jesus would host a Passover (or Passover-like) meal, proclaiming that this was his body and blood as well as asking the guests to do this until he comes again.

This must have been a strange meal indeed, for John's Gospel (in contrast to the other three) keeps it in the background, putting in the foreground the story of the host's washing the feet of the guests (John 13). The contrast between John and the other Gospels on this score is a reminder of how important it is to read the whole of the Gospel dramas rather than isolate any single word or deed of Jesus. Only so can we learn from these Gospels one way that eating and drinking in Jesus' name become what they do not seem to be — power as service of the lowly is inseparable from bread as Christ's body. Indeed, it is only by discerning this movement between the Gospels that we can understand debates in the early church — including debates about why they should go to church, about why this church should assemble. For example, what Paul calls "the Lord's Supper" (1 Cor. 11:20) was scandalously disordered in at least one of Paul's churches: "when the time comes to eat, each of you goes ahead with your own supper, and one goes hungry and another becomes drunk" (1 Cor. 11:21). Paul draws the ironic conclusion that they must not "really" be gathered to eat the supper. Betrayal, it seems, was not only an ingredient of Jesus' supper before his death but also after Pentecost in the suppers of these early churches. But Paul does not threaten withdrawal. Instead, he reminds them of the tradition handed to him and asks them to examine themselves, for "all who eat and drink without discerning the body, eat and drink judgment against themselves" (1 Cor. 11:29). Here, then, is another danger of celebrating this supper until Jesus Christ comes: the risk of self-condemnation.

However, as Paul well knew, we are not simply God's creatures, redeemed in Christ under threat of self-condemnation. The tradition handed to Paul was a tradition of remembrance — but a strange sort of remembrance that includes the future. Our thanks and praise as well as our supplications and lamentations have their point, goal, and aim in God's future world of perfect love for which we are created and redeemed. In other words, Christians who celebrate the Lord's Supper are part of a tradition that extends back to God's rest on the sabbath, Israel's Passover, and Jesus' meals and the Last Supper before his death. But this is not a finished and unchanging tradition, for it also looks forward to the marriage supper of the Lamb at the end time (Rev. 19:9). Between these times, "we know that the whole creation has been groaning in labor pains until now; and not only the creation, but we ourselves, who have the first fruits of the Spirit, groan inwardly while we wait for adoption, the redemption of our bodies" (Rom. 8:22–23). This groaning is, in fact, the work of the Spirit, "for we do not know how to pray as we ought, but that very Spirit intercedes with sighs too deep for words" (Rom. 8:26).

There is, of course, much more that needs to be said about the sorts of persons we need to be in order to live and pray in these ways. But the point here is that going to church is part of this larger story about God and Jesus Christ and the Holy Spirit, about our lives as God's creatures who are given the fruits of the earth and who return such gifts as the work of our hands. In still other words, we might say that we go to church because we "are the church" — a church that knows where it is going: to the Lamb's feast of the end time, when all will sing, "Holy, holy, holy, the Lord God the Almighty, who was and is and is to come" (Rev. 4:8). This sort of going to church is indeed part of the larger adventure of gratitude and repentance and love, part of the larger drama of "being the church." If there are no dangers in this larger adventure, there will seem to be little danger when we assemble. And, if going to church is part of this larger adventure, there is less danger we will confuse it with our nation's customs — whether or not those customs ask us to take a restful or entertaining break from our ordinary lives.

But thinking this way, I must also admit that there will always be good reasons for not going to church — perhaps because the church that thus gathers for the end time is hard to find, perhaps because I find it hard to go to that church. That is, if going to church is part of this larger drama of thanks and repentance, of justice and love, there may be enough dangers in our ordinary lives as dispersed disciples to make us doubt that gathering, assembling, and going to church can do much more than embody our failures to "be the church." This larger drama is not enough. We must assemble. But everything depends on what we *do* when we thus go to church. Here is what I mean.

Word and Sacrament

I complained earlier that Christians do not mean the same thing when they speak of going to church because they engage in such diverse and opposing practices in so doing. But a remarkable convergence is emerging about what it is that we *ought* to be doing when we so assemble: eat and drink the bread and wine that proclaim the death of Christ coming. What is this convergence? And where's the danger? At the risk of under-emphasizing the diversity that characterizes Christian assembly, consider the following common patterns.

Gathering in Repentance. We begin our assembly when we set our minds and hearts on gathering with persons we often do not know and with some of whom we would rather not gather. This is clearly not business as usual, unless our ordinary lives include the admission and forgiveness of sin as standard practice. We go to church not to put our churchgoing righteousness on display or to grovel before God. Instead, our hymns of praise enact our communal glorification of the God of love. It is only in the context of such praise that our repentance and pardon — like the self-examination we saw Paul recommend above — are confessions of sin conquered by one who has staked his identity on forgiveness.

The Word of the Lord. After this transition from our everyday lives to the life of the gathered community, we read and listen to Scriptures proclaimed — the *liturgy of the Word* it is sometimes called. Here we listen to the Scriptures not as mere documents of the past or enunciations of human wisdom in the present — although Scriptures are surely both. But we gather — like Israel on Sinai or after the exile, like Jesus in the synagogue or the church after Pentecost — to hear these Scriptures as the very Word of God. And we gather not only to hear what God's Word says to us as individuals but also what the scriptural readings say to us as a community. Here too is real danger because

God's Word sometimes consoles us and sometimes criticizes us, consoles some and criticizes others.

It is as dangerous to avoid the consolation as the criticism, and much could be said here about the gifts and virtues it takes to thus proclaim the Word of God, a word proclaimed as much in the hearing as in the preaching. But, rather than here discuss how we can discern the spirit in the letter of Scripture, we need to clear the ground of a controversy mentioned earlier. For some Christian communities (let's call them *evangelical*), proclaiming the Word of God is the primary or even exclusive reason for gathering the dispersed community — whereas for other Christian communities (let's call them *Catholic*), the proclamation of Scripture is often a dispensable preliminary to the communion of bread and wine. All too often Catholics assemble less to hear the Word of God than to eat the bread of life — just as evangelicals all too often come to identify the Lord's Supper with making their church too Catholic.

But such choices between evangelical and Catholic communities are choices none of us should wish to make. Recalling the sentence with which I began this essay, our eating and drinking *proclaim* the death of the Lord until Jesus Christ comes again only if our *actions* are thoroughly informed by *words* that proclaim. Saint Augustine called sacraments "visible words," and medieval theologians insisted on the importance of the verbal "form" (the words) as well as the "matter" (bread and wine) of sacraments like the Lord's Supper. Indeed, if evangelical communities need to take more seriously the mandate to regularly eat and drink the supper, Catholic communities need to take more seriously that this is indeed a proclaiming in word of the one who has promised to come again. We might go so far as to say that Scriptures rightly proclaimed can lead the community to communion, whereas communion alone uninformed by the scriptural word can lead in any number of directions, not all praiseworthy, since we eat and drink for any number of reasons — many of them (as Paul warned) confusing our supper with the Lord's Supper.

Thanks and Petition. The importance of proclamation in words is clear in Christian practice as Christians gather for the purpose of listening to and for the Word of God read and preached. But it is also clear as we respond to God's Word with our own words in what is called the *eucharistic prayer* — that is, the thanksgiving prayer. This prayer is modeled on prayers of blessing from the Jewish tradition I mentioned earlier. We hear echoes of this Jewish tradition when the Gospels tell the stories of Jesus' blessing the bread before feeding the crowds, when the introductions to Paul's letters thank God for the communities he addresses. When Jesus took the bread, blessed it, and gave it to his disciples, saying "Take and eat, for this is my body," he was engaged in a replaying of this Jewish tradition. We remember Jesus' blessing as we thank God for all God has done and call upon God to complete this work, transforming us and our food into a meal of memory and promise. Without these words our deeds are empty (much as Gospels of Jesus' deeds without his words would be quite different).

Following on Jesus' creative fidelity, early and later Christians have created a number of versions of this prayer. There is only space here to mention two elements of this praying — patterns that recapitulate patterns of praying we saw earlier. First, the eucharistic prayer will ordinarily include thanksgiving to God for creation and redemption as well as for Jesus Christ, who left the sacrament as the most important memory we need to shape our lives. The risk here is that in gathering our thanks in one prayer, we will remember only the trivial things for which we are thankful. But this particular thanksgiving is embedded in particular memories. *Memory* here is not a vague recollection of an ever-receding past. In fact, the Eucharist heals such vague memories, overcoming our forgetfulness, providing us with the primary one we need to remember: the presence of Christ crucified and risen and coming again in our midst.

Second, eucharistic prayer includes an invocation of the Holy Spirit as well as prayers for the entire Christian community. Indeed, for Greek and Russian Orthodox Christians, the prayer that calls upon the Spirit (called, in Greek, the *epiklesis*) to transform the assembly and the food has always been more central than it has for Catholics and Protestants. The Eucharist is not only thanksgiving and memorial but also a petition. It is not only thankful response to God's mighty acts past and present but hopeful prayer for future mighty acts — a request (as the

Lord's Prayer says) that the kingdom God has promised will come. This prayer for the Spirit is the most powerful expression of protest internal to the Eucharist, the assembly's participation in what we earlier called the groaning of the Spirit for the end time. The *epiklesis* is the cry of hope that the Spirit is shaping the assembly and its food into the people and food of God's reign — the food and drink of this present world a sacrament or epiphany of the food and drink of the coming future. Here our hope is enacted that we are changed into the body of the Jesus Christ in whose memory we pray.

Communion. This eucharistic prayer climaxes in the community's affirmation of the truth of this thanks and prayer: Amen. Only then, informed by the eucharistic prayer (itself a response to the scriptural word), does the assembly eat the bread and drink the wine in communion with Christ and each other for the sake of all the nations. Our communion in this bread and wine that is the body and blood of Christ may be unseemly (tasteless) to a world for whom communion in body and blood is communion in violence. But here our nonviolent (vegetarian!) food proclaims a sacrifice that overcomes our violent sacrifices: Christ crucified and coming. We eat (says an ancient Christian maxim) not to change Christ into ourselves but to be transformed into Christ's body, crucified and glorified.

Sending or Dismissal. The conclusion of our gathering is a prayer sending us forth or giving us a mission — to "go forth in the name of Christ," to "go in peace to love and serve the Lord," to "go forth into the world, rejoicing in the power of the Spirit" (as the *Book of Common Prayer* variously puts it). The rhythm of Word and sacrament commissions us for the life of prayer and action sketched in the previous section. We do well to remind ourselves, however, that this convergence among Christians in eucharistic theory and practice continues to be attended by differences and oppositions. For example, the increasingly common Christian confession of a genuine sacramental presence of Christ *in the eating and drinking* is challenged by those Eastern Orthodox and Roman Catholics who also confess such a sacramental presence *in the bread and wine themselves.* On the other hand, some Reformed and Baptists worry that any talk of sacramental presence (whether in the whole eucharistic practice or also in the bread and wine) overemphasizes the distinctiveness of Christ's presence in the supper at the expense of Christ's real presence elsewhere. Again, while Christians largely agree on the need for ordained ministers of the Eucharist arising *from* as well as able to speak *against* the church, Orthodox and Roman Catholic churches teach the necessity of priestly ordination of men alone, while most other churches have begun ordaining women. Churches agreeing with each other on such issues now find themselves communing together or on the verge of so communing; churches that disagree on what they regard as matters of substance find themselves professing that we are not yet ready for such intercommunion. This is not the place to explain, much less try to resolve, such mutual dissents among Christians. However, such dissents ought to remind us that the less convergence there is toward a common eucharistic supper, the more we are subject to one of the objections with which we began: that going to church is a mask for conflicting practices, and we are like the community in Corinth we heard Paul chide. We celebrate the Eucharist as factions, and therefore some of us do not "really" celebrate Jesus Christ's supper. Perhaps we gather, but with no sense of the danger; or perhaps we prefer the adventure as dispersed disciples, avoiding the danger of assembly. In either case, Christians as a whole do not practice an intelligible answer to our question. Like the Corinthians, we risk eating and drinking unto our own self-condemnation. Can no more be said?

God's Claim on Our Time

The church prayerfully dispersed throughout our neighborhoods and nation-states gathers together, and it is this gathering that feeds us for our lives dispersed throughout those neighborhoods and nation-states. Assembling to celebrate Christ's supper as the Eucharist is a practice in ordinary time — dangerous both because of what it proclaims about this ordinary time (i.e., that this is the time of Christ's death until he comes in glory) and what we proclaim in the shabby ways we enact it (e.g., the self-condemnation of communion that does not proclaim Christ or the proclamation that does not eat Christ's body and drink his blood). The dangers of accommodation and isolation with which I began are pale reflections of the dangers of a mission to transform ordinary time in the light of Christ's coming and the self-condemnation we enact as we fail to do so. Are we left, then, perched between such a litany of dangers to be embraced or avoided?

Thus far I have not sufficiently focused on what is at stake in both "being the church" and "going to church." In Jane Redmont's *Generous Lives: American Catholic Women Today*, Marlene Jones tells the story of being the only African Americans in a local congregation:

> People wouldn't sit next to us. People wouldn't talk to us. My father, being the staunch Catholic that he was, believed that "You don't go to church to serve man; you go to church to serve God. Therefore you will go to Mass on Sundays whether these people acknowledge you or not." So we did. (p. 21)

Some might wonder why Mr. Jones did not shop around to find a more friendly congregation. I suspect that there were simply no nonracist gatherings around. But, even if there were some nonracist gatherings, there would have surely not been communities untainted by serious sin. If it would not have been black and white, it would have been male and female, rich and poor, slave and free, hungry and well fed, weeds and wheat. We might also wish to deny the part of Mr. Jones's claim that said we "don't go to church to serve man." Surely he and his daughter performed heroic service for their fellow Christians and non-Christians — the refusal to identify where the church *is now* and where the church *is going*, a protest from within, because that is where God is.

In any case, most of us are not in a position to quibble with Mr. Jones, for his theological priorities are right. Indeed, he has caught the drift of the commandment to remember the sabbath. This remembrance is not simply going to church or even being the church but assembling before God in response to God — or, better, we are and become the church as we assemble and reassemble before God's unfailing promise to be with us when we gather in Jesus' name, praising God and praying in the Spirit for transformation of us and our world. And here is the central danger of going to church: here *God* calls us together in Word and sacrament, and in so assembling we risk meeting this *God*. This is a dangerous moment of a larger adventure, for here Christ assembles his people for self-examination, for preaching and heeding God's Word, for eating and drinking this one's supper as thanksgiving to the Father and prayer for the Spirit to give us life, for service to God and neighbor.

The Seventh-Day Adventists I briefly mentioned earlier provide a seemingly trivial but nonetheless important challenge to mainstream Christians in this regard. We should gather (they propose) to follow God's command to keep holy the sabbath; God's claim on our time is, in this instance, not a claim on our Sundays but our Saturdays. Mainstream Christians too easily recall Jesus' often harsh criticisms of the way the sabbath command was followed in his time (Matt. 12:1–8; Mark 3:1–6); we find it more difficult to recall that Jesus remembered the sabbath by regularly participating in its practices of prayer and teaching, despite his criticisms.

There are, I think, good reasons to conserve regular Sunday assembly — both because this is the day of Jesus' resurrection and because we can thus join in "protest against the servitude of work and the worship of money" (as the *Catechism of the Catholic Church* puts it). But Seventh-Day Adventist arguments are, I think, admirable efforts to resist accommodation to our culture's claims on our time in contrast to God's claim on that time. To the litany of dangers mentioned throughout this essay I should add another: that our ordinary lives, alone and together (personal and political), will be defined by the rhythms of our ordinary (perhaps, in Nietzsche's deadly sense, eternally recurring) days — that Catholic communities (like my own) will accept their eucharistic practice as a matter of course and that evangelical communities (perhaps using Catholic abuse as an excuse) will make such a celebration the exception rather than the rule. Here the danger is that all of us will miss what we are called to embody in our lives and deaths, in our prayers and meals: the crucified Christ's coming in glory to welcome us into communion with the Triune God and each other.

For Further Reading

Cantalamessa, Raniero. *The Eucharist: Our Sanctification*. Rev. ed. Trans. Frances Lonergan Villa. Collegeville, Minn.: Liturgical Press, 1995. A preacher to the papal household reflects on eucharistic themes.

Eskenazi, Tamara C., Daniel J. Harrington, and William H. Shea, eds. *The Sabbath in Jewish and Christian Traditions*. New York: Crossroad, 1991. Essays by Jews and Christians, including Seventh-Day Adventists, on the sabbath.

Faith and Order Commission. *Baptism, Eucharist, and Ministry*. Faith and Order Paper No. 111. Geneva: World Council of Churches, 1982; and *Baptism, Eucharist, and Ministry 1982–1990. Report on the Process and Responses*. Faith and Order Paper No. 149. Geneva: World Council of Churches, 1990. The most important and controversial of recent documents by a wide variety of Christian churches and communions expressing a convergence in teaching and practice.

Heron, Alasdair I. C. *Table and Tradition*. Philadelphia: Westminster, 1983. A Reformed theologian's history and theology of the Lord's Supper.

Schmemann, Alexander. *The Eucharist: Sacrament of the Kingdom*. Trans. Paul Kachur. Crestwood, N.Y.: St. Vladimir's Seminary Press, 1988. A Russian Orthodox theologian takes the reader on a eucharistic journey.

7

WHY CARE ABOUT THE UNITY
OF THE CHURCH?

Michael Root

A wedding: a young couple entering a new life together, a happy occasion for the families of each. But there is a complication. The groom and his family are devout Catholics; the bride's, moderately active Presbyterians. The young woman, who never before had shown much enthusiasm for church, finds herself attracted by Catholic worship, takes instruction, and is received into the Catholic Church a month before the wedding. Her parents are a bit surprised but certainly do not object. The couple want their wedding to be a mass. The question is tactfully put to the priest: "Might it be possible for the Protestant relatives of the bride also to partake of communion?" The answer is friendly, but firm: no. A note of awkwardness thus intrudes into what should be a celebration of unalloyed joy. When it is time to receive communion, one side of the church comes forward, the other side for the most part remains seated. At the reception afterward, questions are asked: "What keeps the churches apart? Why must division continue in such an irritating way?"

An adult Sunday school discussion in a Lutheran church: the theme is a series of ecumenical proposals for "full communion" with the Reformed and Episcopal churches. The pastor leading the session has some difficulty presenting the complex theological material: the real presence of Christ in the Lord's Supper, episcopal succession, the nature of communion among churches. Discussion is difficult and cramped. After a half hour, a question cuts through the complications: "Why is the church wasting its time with this stuff? We should focus on the important things: evangelism, feeding the hungry, addressing the real problems in our town. Church-unity talks are just rearranging the deck chairs on the *Titanic.*" The comment finds much sympathy in the group (and not a little silent sympathy from the pastor).

These two experiences of church division and the pursuit of unity are not uncommon in contemporary American Christianity. Is division a scandal at the heart of the life of Christ's body? Or is it an institutional irrelevance as long as the churches live in mutual respect and abandon the polemics of an intolerant past? Is the ecumenical movement that seeks the greater visible unity of the church the "great new fact in the history of the church" in the twentieth century, as the historian Jaroslav Pelikan has said? Or is it the ecclesiastical expression of that bureaucratic giantism that we find so threatening in politics and the economy?

The starting point for this essay is less a well-defined "everyday question" in search of an answer than a puzzlement whether an important question lies here or not. Why should we care about the unity of the church? To address this puzzlement, I will need to discuss some basic features of Christian belief about God and salvation, both in terms of their biblical basis and their meaning. Against the background of these beliefs, I hope that we can better understand our present situation.

The One Community

The creation of a reconciled community is intrinsic to the ministry of Jesus as presented in the Gospels. In all four Gospels, the calling of disciples, the creation of a kind of community, stands at the beginning of Jesus' ministry (Mark 1:16–20 and pars.; John 1:35–51). That twelve of these followers are singled out to play a special role is symbolically significant. The Twelve are to sit on thrones and judge the tribes of Israel (Matt. 19:28). In such a selection for such a purpose, the claim is being made that the community of Israel is being renewed and purged in the ministry of Jesus and the reign of God that is breaking in with him. The reign of God that Jesus announces is not just a new relation between God and individuals, for the renewal of communal life is an essential aspect of what Christ does.

In his words and, more strikingly, his deeds, Jesus presents the community as reconciled, as transcending old boundaries and including those who were previously excluded. This community includes "tax collectors and sinners" (Matt. 11:19). The call to this community is a call to repentance, but the harshest of Jesus' words are directed, not at those who seem the greatest sinners, but at those who see no need for their own repentance, at those who thank God that they are not like "other people" (Luke 18:11). This reconciled community is witnessed to and realized in Jesus' table fellowship with the excluded, an action that seems to have created particular offense.

The church's postresurrection proclamation continues to emphasize the creation of such a reconciled community. Especially for Pauline theology, the death of Christ makes possible the creation of a reconciled community of Jew and Gentile:

> Now in Christ Jesus you who once were far off have been brought near by the blood of Christ. For he is our peace; in his flesh he has made both groups into one and has broken down the dividing wall, that is, the hostility between us. He has abolished the law with its commandments and ordinances, that he might create in himself one new humanity in place of the two, thus making peace, and might reconcile both groups to God in one body through the cross, thus putting to death that hostility through it. (Eph. 2:13–16)

However we interpret this difficult passage, it is clear that reconciliation into a single community, "one new humanity," is close to the heart of what was accomplished in the cross.

For Paul, this unity was to be lived out both locally and in the wider church, and much of his correspondence addresses the difficulties of unity. He has heard that in Corinth "there are divisions among you" (1 Cor. 11:18). The Lord's Supper is not celebrated as a feast of unity, but "one goes hungry and another becomes drunk" (v. 21). In the context of the chapter, it is clear that what Paul calls "discerning the body" (v. 29) involves the recognition and respect for communal unity.

Similarly, Paul is deeply concerned with the unity of the wider church. Paul's letters are our most important witnesses to one of the church's first ecumenical crises: the dispute whether Gentile Christians must be circumcised. The dispute precipitated an ecumenical crisis because it touched the realization of communal unity. Paul rebukes Peter precisely when he withdraws from table fellowship with uncircumcised Gentile Christians (Gal. 2:12). For Paul, Peter is here rebuilding the dividing wall Christ had broken down. This confrontation seems to have been one moment in an ongoing tension between the communities with many Gentile members led by Paul and the communities closely related to Jerusalem. Strikingly, however, Paul goes to great efforts to preserve unity with the Jerusalem church. A thread running through many of Paul's letters and through much of Acts is the collection in Paul's churches for the "poor in Jerusalem." Whatever else it was, this collection was an ecumenical act of community (of *koinonia*, as Paul himself says in 2 Cor. 9:13) with what we would call the *mother church*. It was an act that signified the unity of the church, despite the tensions that existed.

Communion in God and with One Another

A central task of theology is not just to establish that biblical concepts interrelate in certain ways but also to seek to understand why they do so. Why is our salvation in Christ inherently communal? How does that communal character relate to the unity of the church?

A guidepost for us here is the New Testament concept of *koinonia*, especially as this concept has been taken up in recent ecumenical theology. This word can be translated various ways, but most often it means something like "communion," "community," or "sharing." How this concept relates both to salvation and to community is important.

In the New Testament, salvation is not simply a benefit persons receive from God. If it were, the relation between God and the person would remain a merely external one between giver and recipient. Rather, salvation is a true communion or fellowship with God. As is said in 1 John, "our *koinonia* is with the Father and with his Son Jesus Christ" (1 John 1:3). Even more strongly, this communion or fellowship with God is a participation in the life of God. A community of persons is not foreign to the being of God but is of God's very nature as Trinity, as the unity of Father, Son, and Spirit. As the unity of the Trinity in love, the life of God is such that it is "participable:" it is open to participation. Our salvation is inseparable from our unity with Christ in the Spirit. It is by dying and rising *with Christ* that one passes into new life. If we are truly in Christ and the Spirit, however, then our relation to God is no longer simply external. When we address God as "Abba," the Spirit is bearing witness with our spirit (Rom. 8:15–16). When we pray, the Spirit is praying with us (Rom. 8:26); that is, our prayers are taken into the relation between the Spirit and the Father. The new life that is (and, more emphatically, will be) our salvation is bound up with this participation in God, as is graphically depicted in the closing chapters of Revelation. God will not just be worshiped in the New Jerusalem: God "will dwell with them as their God; they will be his peoples and God himself will be with them" (Rev. 21:3). The inhabitants of the city "will see [God's] face"; they will "need no light of lamp or sun, for the Lord God will be their light" (Rev. 22:4–5). Against the background of such language, the assertion in 2 Peter 1:4 that through the promises of God we "may become participants of the divine nature" seems less outlandish and more of a piece with other strands in the New Testament.

The passage quoted above from 1 John, however, does not just refer to communion with God. The entire sentence reads: "We declare to you what we have seen and heard so that you also may have *koinonia* with us; and truly our *koinonia* is with the Father and with his Son Jesus Christ." Our communion with God implies our communion with one another. That we are taken up into communion with God, a communion that reconciles us with God, means also that we enter communion with one another in God. The link between this participation in the unity or communion of the Trinity and the communion among persons within the church is most clearly seen in Jesus' prayer in John 17. Jesus prays to his Father that "they may be one, as we are one" (v. 11). More than an analogy is implied. Later Jesus prays, "As you, Father, are in me and I am in you, may they also be in us, so that the world may believe that you have sent me. The glory that you have given me I have given them, so that they may be one, as we are one" (vv. 21–22). A close juxtaposition is established in this passage among three elements: the unity of the Father and the Son, the unity of Jesus with those for whom Jesus prays, and the unity among those for whom Jesus prays. Those who are one with Christ and thus one with the Father through Christ must also be one with each other. The unity of those in Christ reflects the unity of God, "so that the world may believe." This communion of those in Christ with God and with one another is the life of the church.

The interrelation between our saving communion with God and our communion with one another in Christ makes clear why salvation is inherently communal. Salvation is "God with us" in that salvation is a participation in the blessing of God's life, a life that is a perfect unity of love. As a unity of love, and thus already in a sense a relation among persons, that unity now takes into its own life those who are in Christ. Those taken into that divine community themselves become a community. We are one with each other because we are one in Christ and the Spirit. The close interrelation between unity with God and unity with others in God can be seen in the central sacraments of the church: baptism and the Eucharist or Lord's Supper. Each mediates our communion with God and also our communion with one another. From Pentecost on, baptism is the central rite of entrance into the fellowship of the church. Acts 2:41 simply equates being baptized with being added to the community. But to be baptized, as Paul emphasizes, is also to be joined with Christ: "As many of you as were baptized into Christ have clothed yourselves with Christ" (Gal. 3:27). Similarly, Paul says of the Eucharist that the cup of blessing and the bread we break are a sharing (a *koinonia*) in the blood and body of Christ (1 Cor. 10:16). Yet, as noted above, the argument of 1 Corinthians 10–11 is that this community with Christ is also necessarily a communion with others in Christ. The statement that one cannot say, "I love God," and also hate one's brothers and sisters (1 John 4:20) is thus not simply a statement about the ethical implications of Christian faith. It rather expresses the interrelation of our community with God and with others in God.

Unity and Division

How does this discussion of salvation and communion relate to our concrete experience of unity and division? We can get back to the problems that set this essay under way by three steps, each of which extends what has been said so far. First, if this communal life is inseparable from salvation and salvation is a gift of God's grace, then this communal life is also a gift of grace, given in such events as the sacraments. It is not something we create by our mutual love or efforts toward community, however important this love and these efforts may be.

Second, the community inseparable from God's grace has unity as one of its essential characteristics. Paul asks, "Has Christ been divided?" (1 Cor. 1:13), with the implied answer that such is impossible: "There is one body and one Spirit" (Eph. 4:4). The New Testament does speak of churches in the plural, and the theological tradition has affirmed that the various local churches are each *church* in the full sense of the word. Nevertheless, these churches are realizations of the one church, which as the body of the one Christ can only be one.

Third, this community will continue to exist until the return of Christ. In Matthew's Gospel, when Peter confesses Jesus to be the Christ, the Son of the living God, Jesus responds that "on this rock I will build my church, and the gates of Hades will not prevail against it" (Matt. 16:18). This statement (and others, such as the promise in John 16:13 of the Spirit who will lead into all truth) has been generally held to imply the indefectibility of the church; that is, the church will not so depart or "defect" from Christ and the Spirit that it ceases to be the church. This indefectibility is not a function of any special virtue on the part of the church but is a function of God's strength and faithfulness in maintaining the church.

Taken together, these three conclusions imply that the unity of the church is a reality we cannot destroy. A person or community can leave this unity but cannot divide it. This conclusion has almost always been affirmed by the varying Christian traditions. The nature of this given unity is disputed, but that there *is* such a given unity is not. But this conclusion seems to contrast sharply with our present experience. We live out our Christian lives in churches that are not just distinct from each other but that live in separation, as the wedding story at the opening of this essay illustrated. Many do not fully recognize each other as churches; many are unable to celebrate the Eucharist together; many disagree about essential characteristics of the one gospel. We are now back where we started: What do we make of the present division of the church?

In two quite different ways, one might conclude that no truly significant problem (or at least no problem about unity) arises from the apparent contradiction between, on the one hand, what theologically *must* be true about the church and its unity and, on the other, the divisions we seem to experience. First, one might insist that because there is only one church of Jesus Christ, division or separation within the church is simply impossible. There may be distinct churches in the sense of particular congregations or distinct local churches, but these form one unity. When a division occurs, it is always division or separation *from* the one church, never a division *within* it. As a result, if two groups of Christian communities are divided from one another, then only one of these groups can truly be *church*. If both were, then the indestructible unity of the church would be destroyed, which cannot occur. If the present situation constitutes a problem, it is not a problem about unity. It is a problem about identifying the true church and convincing all Christians of good will to join it.

Such an outlook is perfectly consistent and has been widely (if often unreflectively) held in the past. Nevertheless, it has become increasingly hard to accept. In fact, no major Christian tradition (with the possible exception of the Orthodox) insists that it alone is the church. (The Roman Catholic Church, for example, recognizes the Orthodox churches as churches.) Perhaps more decisively, the assertion that all Christian communities but one's own are not churches has become implausible for an increasing number of Christians. Survey data show that American Christians have far more experience of worship and life in other churches today than fifty years ago and that the greater such contact across church borders, the more positive the opinion of other churches. It is doubtful whether the assertion that communities outside one's own are also outside the one church is a believable assertion for many today.

A second perspective takes an almost opposite view. The present division of the churches might be seen as irrelevant to true unity in Christ. For example, one might see unity as completely realized in the common presence of the Holy Spirit in the hearts of believers or the common acceptance of a core of fundamental beliefs. For such a view, the fact that Baptists and Lutherans cannot recognize each other's baptisms or that Catholics and Presbyterians cannot celebrate the Lord's Supper together may be an evil or at least something regrettable, but it has nothing to do with unity. Such a view is, I would guess, widely shared among American Christians, certainly among Protestants, perhaps also among Catholics. We are sisters and brothers in Christ; other churches are churches too, in their own ways (whatever that might mean). The divisions among the churches are bad, especially if they lead to intolerance, but diversity in the religious market is probably a good thing. Most churches are already one in what really counts.

This second view has its attractions: it provides a basis for a friendly coexistence among the churches and makes possible extensive forms of cooperation. Such friendliness is certainly preferable to wars of religion or to the sharper antagonisms of a century ago. The frustrated participant at the Lutheran Sunday school in my story above perhaps spoke out of this perspective. But such a separation of unity from the lived relations among the churches is simply not biblically or theologically acceptable. It divides our unity in Christ and the Spirit both from the Word and sacraments that mediate the foundation of that life and from the events in which that life is concretely lived out.

The problem of such a division is most clear in relation to the Eucharist. As already noted, according to Paul, the cup and bread are communion with Christ and with each other. The entire thrust of his argument in 1 Corinthians 10–14 is that a deep contradiction exists between the theological significance of the meal the Corinthians celebrate and the manner of their celebration. Their lack of concern for each other contradicts the communion of the meal.

Neither of the denials of the problem succeeds. The contradition of unity and division remains. We are in fact one. Christian faith requires such a belief, and we experience this oneness often when we share in the life of a church other than our own. And yet, we are divided. We live in contradiction, a contradiction that cuts to the heart of the church's life. If Christ comes to break down the walls of division and fails to do so even within his own church, then is the gospel simply false? Can our detour through the concepts of salvation, community, and communion help us grasp the nature of this contradiction and answer the question of its importance? What is needed is a clearer sense of how we are one and how we are divided. In trying to spell out more precisely how we are one and yet divided, I must draw on some assumptions specific to my own Lutheran tradition. Nevertheless, I believe arguments to similar effect could be made within the terms of other traditions.

As already discussed, it is a common assertion that the church and its unity are a gift of God, given in and through certain events, most fundamentally in and through the proclamation of the gospel and the celebration of the sacraments of baptism and the Eucharist. Because Word and sacrament mediate Christ's Spirit in which we are one, a certain communion in Word and sacrament, a sharing in the same gospel and the same sacraments, is necessary for unity. Most (but not all) of the Christian tradition has held that a necessary condition of a community's being a church is that it proclaim the gospel and celebrate the sacraments of baptism and the Eucharist in a minimally adequate way (so that their identities as gospel, baptism, and Eucharist are preserved). These are the means by which the gift of life in Christ is given, and so, without these, a community cannot be a church. The strong sense that we are one, even in our divisions, is rooted in the perception that we are in fact proclaiming the same gospel and celebrating the same sacraments.

But Word and sacrament are not important in themselves; they are important because they mediate Christ and the Spirit. Christ and the Spirit are active in those who accept them in faith. They press toward a common life. In 1 Corinthians 12, Paul discusses the various gifts the Spirit gives within the community, but these gifts are to work together for the good of the one body: "There are varieties of gifts, but the same Spirit; and there are varieties of services, but the same Lord; and there are varieties of activities, but it is the same God who activates all of them in everyone" (vv. 4–6). The gift of unity, because it is unity in Christ and the Spirit, has its own inner dynamic toward lived unity. *Because* we are one in Christ, we are called and moved by the one Spirit to live out our unity in a truly common life in Christ. What form such a common life should take is much discussed. Hardly anyone wants simply to erase the diversity of styles of Christian worship, prayer, and theology. There is no reason why Baptists, Episcopalians, and the Orthodox need to give up their quite distinct ways of being Christian. Nor is the idea of a single church bureaucracy very attractive. But the churches are called to a common witness to the one faith and to a sharing in those fundamentals that make them churches. This common witness and sharing mean at least the possibility of a common proclamation of the Christian message and a common celebration of the sacraments. The unity we are given in Word and sacrament has its own inner dynamic toward such a common life; such a common life is the living realization of the unity we are given.

It is this common life, however, that is realized in our churches only in part. We can understand the contradiction of unity and division as the halting of a movement or trajectory before that movement or trajectory has reached its natural goal. We are given a unity in Christ and the Spirit but fail to live out that unity in the way unity itself demands. It has been the more intense experience of this contradiction over the last century that has given rise to the ecumenical movement of the twentieth century. Many ecumenical discussions have reached a promising but precarious stage in which many churches can recognize a range of other churches as being truly churches, proclaiming the one Word and celebrating the true sacraments, but the disagreements are still such that the way to a common life in these foundational realities remains barred. The ecumenical difficulty is that churches that understand themselves to be preaching the same gospel and celebrating the same sacraments judge themselves unable conscientiously to preach and celebrate them together.

Why Care?

How important is this contradiction? It was this question that was posed at the outset and that still awaits an explicit answer. After all, Christians and their churches fail to live out their calling in all sorts of ways. We should avoid placing legitimate priorities in competition with each other, but some weighing of relative significance is unavoidable.

If this failure to live out a common life were limited to matters somewhat peripheral to the center of the faith, for example, disagreement over minor matters of church administration, then perhaps this lack would be only a kind of moral failing, something we should do something about but which does not raise deep problems. The problem becomes more intense, however, when we cannot live out our unity in those events that mediate that unity, in Word and sacrament. While, as noted above, the shared conviction has been that this unity is a gift from God the church cannot lose, this lack of communion cannot leave this unity unaffected. How this effect is to be understood is unclear (and perhaps, like sin, must remain unclear). In a recent letter of the (Roman Catholic) Congregation for the Doctrine of the Faith, Cardinal Joseph Ratzinger finally had to speak metaphorically of this lack of communion, saying it *wounded* churches in their identity as churches, even wounding the Catholic Church itself in its universality. It is because our divisions wound our churches in their identity as realizations of the one church of Jesus Christ that unity and a life in communion are something that must concern us.

The reader may wonder, however, why I have not placed more emphasis on the more vivid wounds that arise from the division of the churches, the nonmetaphorical wounds that result from the religious strife between Protestants and Catholics in Northern Ireland or Catholics and the Orthodox in Croatia and Bosnia. I have deliberately refrained from using such examples for two reasons. First, while the division of the churches has at times had disastrous effects in inflaming social hatreds and often has undermined the credibility of Christian witness, the impression should not be given that we should seek unity only to overcome such hatreds or to make mission more effec-

tive. The thrust of this essay has been that division is a problem
in itself. Its negative effects on human relations and Christian
witness flow from its inherent contradiction to Christian faith.

Further, religious conflict of the sort that leads to bloodshed
has, at least for the present, ceased to be typical of the United
States. The vehement and polemical rhetoric of even the recent
American past (e.g., the 1960 Kennedy presidential campaign)
has extensively disappeared as a feature of discussion about
church differences. For most American Christians, the disunity
of the churches is less a problem than simply a part of the institutional landscape. In a society where the market-consumer
nexus is central, the division of the church can come to seem
natural. It is easy to see, for example, Baptist and Presbyterian as analogous to Ford and Honda. If division wounds the
church, we have become anesthetized to the wound's pain.

This anesthesia is reflected in the divergence of our opening
stories. When division forces itself upon us, as on occasions
such as the wedding described, we are disturbed. But the dy-
namics of much of American church life bypasses the problem
of division. Every local church is the realization in its own time
and place of the one church of all times and all places. Yet in the
everyday life of the typical church, how does this reality (or its
lack) come to expression? American Christianity is so splintered
that any parish or congregation shares a full communion in the
fundamentals of the Christian life with only a minority of other
congregations and parishes. Increasingly, church life focuses on
the local congregation to the exclusion of relations even with
other bodies in the same denomination or church. In the long
run, our church life is impoverished, but in the short run we
feel little pain.

Ecumenical discussions can sometimes seem obscure and
trivial because they sometimes *are* obscure and trivial. The exasperation of the Lutheran Sunday school member in the second
story above, an exasperation I have myself often encountered
and sometimes felt, partially reflects this fact. But it perhaps
also reflects the distance between the experience and priorities
of much contemporary church life and the call to be a truly
catholic church. Here, the underlying problem is reflected less
in the questions we ask every day than in the questions we too

seldom ask. The task of theology in such a case is to contrast church life as we live it with the full reality of the Christian life as the Bible and tradition witness to it. For the Christian, neither theology nor everyday life is the final norm; each is subject to the gospel. Sometimes everyday life must call theology away from its academic byways to attend to what is truly decisive. But on occasion theology must also critique the limitations of everyday Christian existence as we pursue it.

If the life of the local church is truly to be the realization at that time and place of the one universal church of Jesus Christ, then we need to find ways in which our communion with all Christians of all times and places becomes a living theme in the everyday life of our churches and in which the absence of that communion becomes a sensed loss. When this occurs, then a concern with unity and communion cannot be far behind.

Why should we care about the unity of the church and the common life that should flow from it? Most simply, because we must care about living out our life in Christ faithfully both as individuals and as Christian communities. It is faithfulness to the gift of communion with God through Christ and the Spirit that should move us to seek the fullness of communion with all those with whom we share that gift.

For Further Reading

Faith and Order Commission. *Baptism, Eucharist, and Ministry.* Geneva: WCC Press, 1982. A good example of ecumenical dialogue, the most widely read and discussed dialogue report.

John Paul II. *Ut Unum Sit* (That they may be one). Papal encyclical on ecumenism. (Can be found in *The Encyclicals in Everyday Language,* Maryknoll, N.Y.: Orbis, 1996.) One of the best recent statements from any church.

Fackre, Gabriel and Root, Michael. *Affirmations and Admonitions.* Grand Rapids: Eerdmans, 1998. Spells out the argument of this essay in more detail.

8

WHAT SHALL PARENTS TEACH
THEIR CHILDREN?

William Werpehowski

Once I became a parent, my first-time answer to this question was pretty conventional. Parents should teach their children to care about others, to know the difference between right and wrong, to learn the value of hard work, and to think for and be true to themselves, rather than merely conform to the pressures of the group. Whatever its merits, the response undoubtedly had much to do with my fears as a father. I was (and still am) afraid that my sons will become selfish oafs or that they will never understand what it means to play by the rules or that they will never land a (good!) job or that they will cave in to this or that improper or dangerous behavior just because it is authorized by the crowd. On reflection, I had to ponder whether I was working with conceptions of success and the rules of life that were themselves an accommodation to the temper of the times that I seemed in many ways to dread. Beginning with apprehensions about my children's safety, did I not come up with ideas about training them that would place them safely within the framework of our commercial culture? Not wanting them bought and sold, I wondered whether my first impressions were about teaching my sons how to sell themselves as dependable, rule-abiding, civil commodities in the workplace. After all, what was I doing leaving the love of God out of the answer? What kind of safety was I really desiring for the boys?

This self-assessment may be too harsh, but the present effort intends to correct the tendency — for surely there was that in some measure — spontaneously to prefer status-quo solutions to the dangers posed by the status quo. The question of this essay also requires a Christian theological response. If I would focus on "what it takes" for children to be grown up in a world created and redeemed by God, I must also be attuned to rethinking "what it takes" in terms of the call to love God and neighbor. Making a living, getting along with others (or even being not just liked but well-liked), and being your own person cannot be certified uncritically as signs of the maturity that parental instruction should strive to foster; for Christians believe that a particular kind of maturity is at stake for human creatures who may come freely to stand in the devoted service of God. That has to be the measure of the meaning and significance of goods like work, sociability, and self-responsibility.

There is a divine commandment that relates to our theme, but at first glance it does not appear to be very useful. Consider the injunction that children shall honor their mother and father. Commentators have lamented its asymmetrical status in the Decalogue. Stephen Post writes: "If one additional commandment could be added to the Decalogue, 'Love thy children' would be a prime candidate. That the Decalogue omits a commandment to love and honor one's children is unfortunate, since in various instances it appears that parental love requires such encouragement. The authoritarian notion that parents have a right to respect or to love simply because they are parents is as erroneous as it is desperate." Post contends that filial love is the child of parental love and that honoring parents should be "the expression of a filial love that is a response to parental love." It would be tyrannical to answer the question, "What shall parents teach their children?" merely with "To honor their mother and father."

There is much to be said for Post's line of thinking. It is true that parents ought to love their children. Statements of parental authority that do not include this requirement are defective. Certainly an important moral issue arises about the possibilities for or necessity of filial piety where, for example, biological parenthood is not complemented by care and nurturance or when a parent constantly neglects his or her children or subjects them to abuse. One does not respond effectively or decently to that issue just by recalling the words of the fourth commandment.

It also makes sense to realize that in many ways parental love shapes and qualifies the love and confidence in others, including parents, that children develop and express.

There is a danger, however, in pushing too far the case for making parental love the condition for honoring one's mother and father. Post sees one side of it when he says that a demand for reciprocity may tempt children to calculate how much filial love to give back. They might even hastily dismiss filial honor altogether, given their parents' failures. Another problem moves in the opposite direction. If it is to be the basis of filial piety, the moral requirement of parental love still vests in parents an enormous authority. Anxious to promote their children's well-being, mothers and fathers may need to battle with fantasies of control over and excessive identification with their children. In the one case they could simply impose desires and disciplines of their own making for the sake of the child; in the second they would project them. Innocent parental strategies, like your trying to attend to a child's needs, can include an intense investment leading to preoccupation with his or her well-being as it reflects your own or to damaging expectations about how he or she should, given your sacrifice, come to love and honor *you*.

Both sides of the danger share in the human urge for self-justification. Thus filial love is conditioned by children's judgment of parents who will fail and fail again. Parental love is bedeviled by a possessiveness that correlates with the massive responsibility of caring for children. The prospect of suffering judgment tightens the parents' grip; the tighter the grip, the more an act of judgment is necessary to liberate children from their parents. Alternatively, the demands of parents who love their children judge *them*, so that the latter, who also fail and fail again, will manage this burden either by succumbing to self-doubt or through exercises of presumption and isolated independence.

But God, not the child, finally measures and judges the work of parents. And children do not belong finally to parents, but to God. Honoring mother and father must be a response to a divine authority to which parents can only witness.

Try to think of the commandment of filial honor in light of the following passage from the Letter to the Ephesians:

Children, obey your parents in the Lord, for this is right. "Honor your father and mother" (this is the first commandment with a promise), "that it may be well with you and that you may live long on the earth." Fathers, do not provoke your children to anger, but bring them up in the discipline and instruction of the Lord." (Eph. 6:1–4)

The injunction to obedience "in the Lord" is immediately interpreted in terms of a promise. To adhere to the command is not a means to the promise's fulfillment, but a form of the fulfillment itself. The point is not that if you obey mom and dad, then you are sure to become a success in the world. It is instead that obedience to mom and dad "in the Lord" may be a constitutive feature of living well and long on the earth the Lord has made. The command to filial honor in this passage refers at once to what children may hope for in their obedience and to what their elder parents have received: the divine assurance that keeping covenant with the Lord is our deepest fulfillment as human creatures. The promise for children is also a reminder to parents of their commission to be faithful to God and to do this, not less, but more than ever in the upbringing of children. Parents are to be honored, as Karl Barth puts it, "as the bearer and mediator of the promise given to the people." Their authority may and shall *bear promise* of God's goodness, and it has validity for no other purpose than this.

Filial respect and obedience are not, therefore, grounded in the fact of biological generation or in mere seniority or in the fine traditions they may embody or in their moral rectitude. Children ought to honor their parents because parents are most fundamentally their teachers who lovingly instruct them by word, deed, and example in the practice of living before God. Generation, seniority, tradition, and character serve this central mission. One cannot permit any of these qualities to stand on its own and thereby vest parental authority with its own self-supporting worth. Even the image of *teachers* is misleading if it is interpreted as either a more distanced imparting of knowledge or as a self-styled shaping of the ignorant in the teacher's own image. No, the lived knowledge of the Word and work of God may be given in a kind of intimate apprenticeship by the apprentice parents themselves. Children heed their parents and give them the respect they are due in this context.

What shall parents teach their children? A good preliminary answer, after all, is that they may teach their children to honor their mother and father. The answer gives no title to authoritarianism or self-congratulation, nor is it conditioned by the requirement of an abstract, independent parental love. Parents may teach children to be *children*, eager and attentive learners about the good, created world in which they live. To that end they might nurture in them a confident neediness and a self-limiting assertiveness that enables good questions, vivid imaginings, and honest assessments of people and things. Good teaching elicits these virtues by example and by a gracious care that entertains vulnerability with hope, not crippling fear. Above all parents establish their authority and teach these virtues by giving their children instruction in the Lord, enthusiastically taking up their vocation as elders yet humbly refusing to grasp privileges and a manner of devotion for themselves that is owed only to God.

On the one hand, if parental authority ever requires, as it does with young children, unreflective obedience, that obedience must be for the purpose of teaching children the way of free responsibility to God. If parents would insist on adjustment to the norms of this or that group (e.g., the scout pack or school or team), that must be because conformity supports and does not encumber the child's maturation as a creature and child of God in Christ. Instruction in the moral verities — tell the truth, play fair, the Golden Rule — should enable one's capacity to look up to but also beyond instruction and the verities themselves, to their source in the divine call to love one's fellows. On the other hand, when we encourage youngsters to think for themselves, we do it in the hope that they will affirm their own insights and powers in fundamental loyalty to God and the neighbor. Should we implore them to stand up for their rights or not to buckle under to peer pressures, we do this to engage a skill that stands fast against corruptions of one's creaturely good and responsibility. Finally, when there is tension and disagreement between parents and children, parents inspire honor and teach its meaning by intending the hard words or the reconciling gestures or the negotiated reciprocal disciplines for children's better understanding of the divine ordering under which *both* disputing parties stand.

It is not easy for a parent at once to embody authority and to refer it away from oneself. An obvious temptation is to identify completely with authority, given that before our kids' eyes we are endowed (at least for a time) with a whole lot of power. Another temptation is a slothful kind of self-removal. Fitting a cultural situation in which people care very much about personal autonomy, one tends to escape real instruction by merely pointing to a variety of commodified options and letting the kids decide. You want them to be "exposed to religion" or "to learn right from wrong"; but all the time you evade your own lived, authoritative relationship to your children and the goods you are bound to share with them. Teaching children to be children and before God to honor their mother and father demands neither tyranny nor high-minded disengagement.

It is not easy for children, moreover, really to honor their parents while and after parents are exposed to be destructive, faithless, and phony. When I was growing up in the 1960s, the charge of "hypocrite" was a personal and generational favorite. Our parents were not spared it, and the charge was not always wrong. Now *I* stand before my children in the dock, awaiting their inevitable naming of my shortcomings as a Christian, a father, a teacher, mom's husband, and so forth. Here is a test for parent and child alike. I hesitate to address the matter since there are extreme and not uncommon examples of parental wickedness that can seem to render the following analysis inappropriate. The point remains that since the authority of parents is based on the grace of the sovereign God, their failures are finally to be referred to God's grace and rule. If weak and sinful parents have been able at all to teach their children what honor of mother and father means, there may be hope that these children will hold them accountable but with at least a touch of patience and gentleness, and without self-righteousness. Parents also cannot wander from their mission and therefore may catch themselves up penitently and redirect their energies to the source of goodness. They will not deny the harm they do, but they also will not despair of the authority entrusted to them.

Children will not look past the vicious ways of their parents, but neither will they abandon their responsibility still to listen and learn, if they can, from them. In both cases there will be a faithful forgetting and recovery of self that is permitted by a mutual understanding of the source and character of the honor that parents are due.

Parents ought to teach children to be children and, as such, to honor their parents as teachers and mediators of a divine promise of redemption in Jesus Christ. But parents should not and cannot do this if they presume to be to their children divine representatives. They are permitted as parents, as Barth says, "to bear witness to the fact that their children exist under the hand of God" and to act on the understanding that Jesus Christ wills to have them as brothers and sisters. Their authority is exercised only as children come to realize that both parents and children stand under divine authority. Parents, therefore, may bear witness by teaching and embodying for their children virtues, dispositions, beliefs, and a way of life that fit the fact that the world is God's world. They teach the love of God and neighbor by loving God and neighbor and by imaginatively sharing and explaining this love with their sons and daughters. They teach the way of the world by seeing and reading it that way themselves with their children in light of the biblical witness and the practices of the Christian community. The reflections in the preceding section are just specific aspects of such seeing and reading of the world given the subject matter of the parent-child relation itself. In the remainder of this essay, I will present four basic dispositions and virtues that parents may learn and learn to teach their children.

Joy

Parents shall teach their children to be joyful. No attitude better reflects the good news of God's reconciling fellowship with us in Jesus Christ. And I fear that no other attitude so readily gets lost in the shuffle of interactions between parents and children. We suppose there may be great joy present with the receiving and welcoming of a newborn into the world, as well as in so much early nurturing. But in time the joyful love may recede in the face of all the many things we are to do in the world. There is so much to do, like schoolwork, popcorn sales, music lessons, soccer practice, the school play. There is so very much to do, like making a living, doing the shopping, raking the leaves, bravely struggling for a decent home, a living wage, a good enough school, a peaceful neighborhood. How can we find the space and the time to be good parents *and* to be joyful?

If we cannot find the space and the time, we cannot effectively teach our children the experience of joy, which is to know and feel some specific fulfillment in our lives as creatures created by and restored to God. It is to take a full breath in grateful acknowledgment that we have received some good that properly ennobles us. We may have prepared for this fulfillment through study, toil, and careful deliberation; yet if our preparation was joyful, if it anticipated the fulfillment properly, then it was constituted by a readiness for receiving the completion as a gift. If parents received their lives as a divine gift and, more to the point, welcomed their children as wondrous and astonishing gifts, their parents' readiness for gratitude should not be an alien disposition.

Gratitude often seems to be alien, however, and we can make it something odd and strange to our kids. Two connected messages, communicated by our words and our lives, contribute to this. First, there is the idea that through hard work we must make something of ourselves, must do something significant with our lives. The trouble here is the suggestion that we are of our own making and that, apart from successful self-making in this or that area, we are, and perhaps *should* be, nothing. This stance orders life to a law of achievement and independence. It afflicts many of my college students with an overwhelming blindness about how dependent and uncontrollable their life situations are and leaves their hearts unready for joy and ready only for the "personal satisfaction" of clearing another hurdle. The second message is put brilliantly by the capitalist restauranteur Pascal in the film *Big Night*. He tells struggling Secondo, with a line that sets him up for a devastating betrayal, "Bite your teeth into the ass of life and drag it to you!" Apparently intended to inspire courage and confidence, the advice warrants a grasping, aggressive orientation. The world is apprehended, not joyfully, but at best with confidence in domination, in doing it "my way." Parents, looking at life not as a created gift but as seductive and threatening, could teach children these things in order to protect them.

Nevertheless, parents shall teach their children to be joyful. They are sustained by God's grace at every moment. They may trust in God's love and mercy as it is given in Jesus Christ. In the satisfaction of their needs, in their fellowship with others, in the exercise of talents that were enabled and nurtured by others, parents should be ready to pause to give thanks and help their kids do likewise. One way to learn this is by keeping the sabbath holy, for on this day human creatures are called not just to rest from toil but to rest for the sake of giving thanksgiving. Far from demanding we make something of ourselves, the sabbath commandment demands we depart from independent reliance on our own work. Far from encouraging or idealizing a predator's grasp of the world, it calls us to renounce our anxious clutchingness.

Within the life of the family, parents may teach their children (and themselves — always themselves) to be joyful by making time together more expansive and less strictly programmed. There is something odd about scheduling time to "stop and smell the roses"; instead parents may sometimes simply be ready to linger with and luxuriate in a four-year-old's endless recounting of his daytime activities or to welcome, not just put up with, a pair of last-minute dinner guests that a child has invited without the parents' knowledge. Finally, we can teach joy in work and service to the neighbor by helping our children see that the other is a gift and not a threat and by enacting the stubbornly hopeful conviction that by grace the unpleasant chore or tense encounter or vicious injustice may be transformed and redeemed.

Keeping Faith

As first of all joyful, children may be summoned to make something of themselves for the sake of God and God's creation. Thus parents shall teach their children to be faithful, to be loyal to God's cause and the cause of the neighbor. Children shall be taught to develop their talents as an expression of this loyalty, to discipline themselves, to understand the joys but also the cost of attaining some excellence in the communities of social practice that answer to human needs and serve the common good.

I want to suggest a contrast with a different proposal that, however well-meaning and insightful, requires correction. The proposal starts, simply and wisely enough, with the claim that children should know themselves to be valuable, special, loved, and at home in the world apart from anything that they do or achieve or fail to achieve. Young people need to have self-esteem and to feel good about themselves. In fact, self-esteem turns out to be the condition of their trusting themselves enough to venture to attain their special abilities in the world. So far, so good. These ideas present important social and psychological truths, especially that children need to possess a sense of fundamental trust in the world and in themselves as actors in it. They must accept themselves as able to establish a secure identity and not be hampered by severe self-doubt. This message also exposes the harm that continual ridicule, harassment, and degradation may inflict on a child. It even touches the field of social criticism, should we join the philosopher John Rawls in holding that a person's self-worth depends on the responses of others and that, therefore, the justice or injustice of democratic institutions can be evaluated for the way they do or do not reflect a citizenry's support for one's reasonable goals and aspirations.

The difficulty is that an emphasis on prior self-esteem and self-acceptance is often tied to an abstract and atomistic view of the human self in which self-esteeming desires, whatever they are, become the independent foundation for all other projects. Human self-understanding, in turn, is based on effectively pursuing and realizing one's preferences, on the one hand, while remaining ultimately unencumbered by them, on the other. The common advice becomes "You have to love yourself before you can love someone else," "You gotta do what you gotta do," or "God wants [here, place your name in the third person] to be happy" (typically stated in explanation for some broken commitment). A modest plea for realistic self-acceptance devolves into an apology for selfishness or at least for a standpoint that

gauges human pursuits in terms of the satisfaction they bring to
the desires of a socially unmoored individual.

Nevertheless, parents may teach their children to be faithful,
loyal to God and the neighbor God loves. Loyalty is living in the
Lord's presence and under God's ordering will. A selfish partial-
ity toward oneself or one's preferred group or ideals is excluded.
But irresponsible flight from freedom in presenting to God one's
particular life and talents is ruled out, too. The human creature stands before God as an individual, yet the identity of the
individual creature is crucially comprised of promises that are
made and fidelities assumed in human communities. Social life
is not something added on to this identity, nor is there any neutral point of desire or choice from which we may choose to be
or not to be with our fellow human being in fellowship. Life
as an individual is a matter of responsible fidelity. I do not
think that this means that our identities are "swallowed up"
in our commitments to others, but it does mean that, however
we preserve ourselves or describe ourselves as individuals before God, preservation and description are always of persons
who are to be with others faithfully in community. We cannot completely tease apart our commitment to ourselves from
our steadfast commitments to others in the practices of church,
family, neighborhood, school, work, play, and so on.

Children shall be taught that a promise is a promise, but also
that not all loyalties are voluntarily chosen but can be assumed
and discovered in the course of life. They may learn such things
in fitting response to the cause of the family and the needs
of its members. Parents should make the home a school for
love and justice in the way they honor and, in hard times, renew their own marital vows, in seeing that household labor is
fairly shared and welcomed by all, in the practice of hospital-
ity toward friends and strangers in need, and in the way family
conflicts are resolved in a peaceable spirit and with reconciling
will. There must be a continuing development of a sense of responsibility for the good of all human beings who claim our
allegiance as brothers and sisters of Jesus Christ. We are to be
loyal to him by our fidelity to them, and often that will mean
keeping our loyalty to other causes as such in a proper order. In
addition, the skills for just complaint should include discerning

when human need is bypassed in the name of some other good improperly loved. After I scolded my younger son for climbing dangerously atop a counter to reach for a snack, his big brother (understanding and not merely noticing that by his fall he had hurt himself) scolded me: "Dad, the *first* thing you should have said is, 'Are you all right?'" He was exactly on target.

In their study, play, and self-development, children can learn to see the connections between their budding dreams, abilities, and individuality and the communal practices, practitioners, and fellows they serve and are served by in turn. Learning about whales says something about being a creature and steward of creation. Playing baseball invites a sense of the history and communal integrity of the game. Vocational training must keep in full view the persons one is to help and the colleagues with and from whom one learns to practice his or her work well. I do not want to advise a tedious and self-defeating moralism whereby every deed begets some lesson and every lesson delivers some law of "right" communal identity. Yet part of the challenge of teaching our children is to elicit comprehension that personal discipline, excellence, and care for others in community are opportunities for a life of freedom. Self-betrayal is betrayal of that freedom, but betrayal of that freedom is being unfaithful to the causes that give us life and to which we adhere.

Teaching children that they may flourish and be free by keeping faith with God and neighbor sometimes strikes me (faithlessly) as being an impossible task. Just like my inability to hit a curveball with any success, my record of keeping faith, and of finding it liberating, hardly inspires self-confidence. In this context the old bromide that "those who can't do, teach" convicts. How really do parents teach the love of God by way of the virtues of humility, trust, and gratitude? How do they help their children understand that blessing may be known in sorrowing over suffering, in gentleness, mercy, peace, and the love of righteousness? Maybe a way to take up these tasks is through participation in the life of the Christian community and particularly in the celebration of the Eucharist. Joined with one another in sharing in the life of Jesus Christ, members of the community gathered to worship him share their embodied commitment to the nonviolent and self-giving peace he gave to us and all humanity. To give thanks for God's creative and redeeming work, to prayerfully hear and reflect on God's Word, and to witness and conform ourselves to Christ's faithful love for the vulnerable and the lost may indicate directions for learning of fidelity that turn wonderful and surprising.

Patience

"Life," John Lennon sings to his son Sean, "is what happens to you while you're busy making other plans." There is a religious version of this idea in a well-known joke that, depending on the delivery and the audience, comes across as either marvelous or mean: "Know how to make God laugh? Tell him your plans." To be joyful means to trust that the world will manifest itself as God's gift, and an implication of this readiness is in fact to sit loose to our designs or to loosen the grip on our life plan or deftly to elude the grip it has on us. To be faithful means, among other things, to keep covenant with persons to whom one is bound, not only by choice but also by circumstances, history, and nature. The unexpectedly sick child or parent, or the student who always tries hard but does not yet quite "get it" — these folks may fittingly claim our faithful response, disrupting our timetables and programs. To be joyful, however, does not mean to overlook evil, and real fidelity often brings us face to face with human suffering and wickedness. Enduring joyfully and faithfully demands patience, the disposition to wait attentively for the good in the wake of difficulty and hardship.

The patient person abides vigilantly in the presence of suffering, injustice, and the many other ways in which the good is vitiated. People are tempted either to be overcome by evil or blithely to discount its threats. Perhaps they get into the habit of losing their kindly equanimity, replacing it with choleric and damning judgment; or maybe they try to guarantee equanimity through an ersatz "tolerance" amounting to a refusal to render and act on moral judgments concerning the good. Christians fail to witness to God in Christ by seeking good results through unfitting, unfaithful means, or they would abandon the redemptive universality of their commitments by despairingly removing themselves from the arena of the world, just leaving it to its own evil devices. In the first instance the problem is deepened by what Thomas Merton called the "fetishism of immediate visible results," whereby a consumerist reluctance to defer satisfaction over moral success works against social transformation by encouraging a sense of futility when easy expectations are dashed. The second alternative replaces easy expectations about good results in the world with an excessively earnest acquiescence about their unlikelihood. So we find that people lose their vision of the emergence of the good in time or that they are not able to wait with integrity for the good they see and hope for.

Yet Christians may be patient, and parents shall teach their children to be patient. When a boy's or girl's best efforts do not bear good fruit, instruction in patience answers the penchant to "have a fit" or to languish in disappointment. When childhood friendships turn sour or cruel, teaching patience, not indifference or forgiveness on the cheap, enables the chance of their restoration in time. To teach revulsion at sin and injustice without the self-righteous embrace of unjust remedies permits a more timeful understanding of the good that we desire. The injunction not to provoke our children to anger but to instruct them in the Lord encompasses forbearing from ridicule, undue harshness, and excessive demands for perfection. Parental wrath can give rise to an anger that refuses to give and to accept the time to learn and to love, as the Lord patiently wills. In learning as teachers to avoid both punitive judgments and moral indifference, parents also hope that they may help their children see that the time they are given should itself give others a time that is gracious. So they should neither oppose nor contemn, for themselves or others, the attainment of any creaturely good; nor may they refuse to measure that good by the fullness of human maturity. If, for example, being popular is important for our children, we should not deny their understanding that recognition and appreciation by others can be a wonderful sign of the achievement of the good. Yet we should add that the good for which we may justly be recognized is of a certain sort. Parents give children time to learn this when they map both the good turn they made and the route they need still to take. And children may learn to be patient by waiting and working expectantly for their destination without presumption or loss of heart.

I have answered impatiently the impatient question, "How long 'til we get there?" many times. And I have asked that question impatiently under many guises: "How long before I'm promoted?" "How long before the kids grow up?" "How long before these people see the error of their ways (and come around to my way of thinking)?" Even the life of prayer can be an opportunity for impatience: "How long before these distractions get out of my head?" "How long before my prayers are answered?" "How long before I get rid of my bad habits?" "How long before I understand what God is up to?" Still I think the practice of prayer, on one's own and with others, can be a kind of schooling in patience. It could be the locus of a tension between sorts of creaturely desires before God — "Father, if you are willing, remove this cup from me; nevertheless not my will, but yours, be done" — that helps us learn how we are located by God and God's ongoing story for us. The distractions that fill us up as we pray afford opportunities, as do the frustration and bafflement, that sense of getting nowhere that can accompany our prayers. When we do not despair and do not succumb to the distractions, or when our confusion reminds us of a helplessness that prompts us further to love God and know God's ways for us, we are getting at something important. Asking God's help in times of trial, where the help one longs for fits the story of peace and self-giving love that is Jesus Christ, is also a form of patience. Parents shall teach their children to be patient, and to that end parents shall teach their children to pray.

Wisdom

Finally, parents shall teach their children to be wise. We must distinguish wisdom from the "prudent" skill to determine the most efficient means to assure one's goals. The virtue of wisdom refers, instead, to the ability to draw certain conclusions from experience about the concrete manner in which we may live well as creatures. It has two related dimensions. There is, first, the habit of discerning the fitting presence and order of goods in specific situations; second, there is the accompanying lived understanding of certain basic truths of our creaturely existence that enable and, in turn, are enabled by the habit of discernment. Age and experience do not automatically make someone wise. Stephen's gentle scolding about my response to James's injury was precisely a lesson taught by one who wisely discerned the order of the good through an understanding of the claims of human need and vulnerability. But as elders, parents hope to teach their children something about the art of living, given their own stumbling and wavering longevity in adherence to God's cause. Perhaps by way of their realizing that joy does not cast a blind eye on suffering or that fidelity to friends and lovers must not be idolatrous or that patience does not fail to hasten but rather includes a sense of urgency about witnessing to God's kingdom, parents can meet their responsibility to their children in this regard.

I close with two stories. Years ago, when Anne and I were beginning to think about day-care arrangements for our one-year-old son, I had a chat with my mother about raising children. I noted, probably with a touch of defensiveness, that our placing Steve in day care would not interfere with our giving him lots of "quality time." Mom thought about this comment and said quietly, "But Billy, remember that children just need time." She was not decrying day care or our career choices. She was pointing out that "quality time" talk and thinking could impede discovering how raising our kids may be more integral to everyday life, and therefore less compartmentalized and idealized. She clinched the point by recalling how, when she was studying long hours for her college degree, she nevertheless took the time to give me time by including me in her time, in her dreams and ideas about her work and her life. At its best, this was an exciting disclosure of subjects that I, only seven or eight years old, could not understand — philosophy, sociology, Cervantes, Shakespeare. Sometimes I spent time with her waiting for her to help me with some problem. Always, I was able to witness devotion to the cause of education. Being let in on the details of her busy life in these ways was different from being given "quality time" after the details were covered. So in recalling this story, Mom took the truism that "children need time with their parents" and showed how it requires caution about not deceiving ourselves as to the way the time we give does and does not properly share our lives with our children.

A few years earlier, my father called me to report that his dad, my eighty-seven-year-old grandfather, had been moved to a nursing home. Racked with severe arthritis, Grandpop could no longer walk on his own. He had also become incontinent. The latter fact made my father confused and angry. His father was a remarkably independent and proud man, and if the first indignity was troubling, the second was cruel. I did not know what to say to help Dad cope with his sadness and irritation. But two weeks later, when we were visiting Grandpop in the nursing home, this is what happened. In the course of a pleasant conversation, Dad noticed that Gramps had "wet his pants." He said, "Pop, we gotta clean you up." The tone, to my surprise, was upbeat, matter of fact. My father had me help him by retrieving clean pants, lifting Gramps out of his wheelchair, taking him to the toilet, getting him redressed, and sitting him back in the chair. Throughout Dad was cheerful and competent. I found no trace of anxiety or pity or revulsion, but I did, I am sorry to say, experience these emotions, only to learn better from him in the course of our mission. When we sat Gramps down, he looked at me with a smile that was pleased and unashamed. He pointed to his son, my father, and told me, "He's a good boy."

My mother taught me wisely about the time our children need by recalling a story about care. My father taught me about the meaning of filial love by embodying it in actions that wisely fit the circumstances of parental need. And in doing so, he carried forward a story — his story — about the nature of love for a parent through the seasons of human life. Wisdom has something to do with recalling stories and carrying them forward, grafting ourselves to them and growing out from them. In the Christian community, the full wisdom of God would be apprehended in a story of creation and fall, covenant, incarnation, self-giving love, suffering unto death, and new life. It is a story that identifies God through the life and ministry of Jesus Christ and in the folly of the cross that he bore for our sakes. If parents are to teach their children what it means to live more humanly and more wisely, they shall teach their children God's story and seek by God's grace to carry it forward with them throughout the time they share together.

For Further Reading

Barth, Karl. *Church Dogmatics,* vol. 3, pt. 4. Edinburgh: T. & T. Clark, 1961. I have relied heavily on Barth's discussions of "Parents and Children" and joy.

Hauerwas, Stanley. *Truthfulness and Tragedy.* Notre Dame, Ind.: University of Notre Dame Press, 1977.

Meilaender, Gilbert. *Letters to Ellen.* Grand Rapids, Mich.: William B. Eerdmans Company, 1996.

Post, Stephen G. *Spheres of Love.* Dallas: Southern Methodist University Press, 1994.

Ruddick, Sara. *Maternal Thinking.* Boston: Beacon Press, 1989.

9

WHAT DOES MY FAITH
HAVE TO DO WITH MY JOB?

William C. Placher

Mary and Ben are both doctors — she's a surgeon; he's a pediatrician. They met in medical school, married during their residencies. They both love their work, and they're good at it. As Christians, they feel grateful that they have jobs in which they are so obviously helping people. But they feel frustrations too. Their jobs call for long hours; caring about their patients takes lots of emotional energy. They joined a local church, but they cannot commit themselves to much involvement, and even Sunday mornings they sometimes find themselves so exhausted that they do not get to church. Saving the lives of other people's children, they spend less and less time with their own.

Dan works in an auto factory. He has a boring job, and he wishes he could find something better. But his daughter Anne was born with a heart condition. Dan's wife has had to stay home and care for her, and Dan is afraid that a new employer's health plan would not cover Anne's existing condition. So he sticks at a job he hates.

Sallie works for an ad agency. She knows how cynical most people are about the advertising business, but it has offered her a chance to write and produce designs just as she had hoped when she was studying English and art in college. And the office is full of interesting and creative people. But she has just been assigned to a new account — a cigarette company. The new job is a promotion, and her boss said she had been chosen for her "youth-oriented point of view." She suspects that means the client wants to target teenagers with this ad campaign, and the idea of getting more kids to start smoking bothers her.

Imagine yourself a pastor, facing Ben and Mary, Dan, and Sallie in your congregation. You have decided to preach a sermon on the relation of faith to a Christian's job. What would you say to them?

Particularly for Protestants, the traditional Christian language for talking about one's job was as a *calling* or *vocation*. When we talk about *vocational counseling*, we are apt to forget that a vocation (the word just means "call" in Latin) was originally something a person was called by God to do. The idea that one can be called to many different sorts of jobs was one of the radical proposals of the Reformation. In the Middle Ages *vocation* generally applied only to those who were called to be priests or nuns or monks. The Reformers disagreed. When angels announced the birth of the Christ child, Martin Luther once reminded his congregation, they did not deliver the news to monks or bishops but to shepherds — honest working folk who were doing their job and thus fulfilling their vocation: "These were real sheepherders. . . . They did what shepherds should do. They stayed in their station and did the work of their calling."

It is too simple, however, to draw a sharp line between Protestant and Catholic views on this topic. Even before the Reformation, groups like the Brethren of the Common Life in the Netherlands were pursuing callings to more deeply religious lives that kept them in their secular occupations. In our own century, the Catholic Church, at the Second Vatican Council, proclaimed that men and women working to provide for themselves and their families and benefiting society "can justly consider that by their labor they are unfolding the Creator's work." They are, in other words, serving God in their vocations. The Reformation emphasis on any job as a calling has become in some measure part of the heritage of all Christians. In some ways it was and still is a radical idea. Every task, Luther said, has fundamentally the same dignity. The shoemaker and the shepherd are responding to their callings and doing God's work just as much as the bishop and the king. This, John Calvin once remarked, is a "singular consolation" to those whose work is "sordid and base." However hard it may be, and however treated with contempt by much of society, what they do is valued by God.

Thinking about our jobs as vocations still has much to recommend it. We often emphasize that we should not be Christians just on Sundays. That means that our faith ought to have applications for our family life, our friendships, and our citizenship as well as our worship. But for many of us, our job takes up a big part of the rest of the week. If our faith is supposed to shape every aspect of our lives, should it not say something about how we think about our work?

Still, does it make sense for the pastor of Ben, Mary, Dan, and Sallie to talk to them about vocation? Dan's job involves hard routines over which he has no control — it is difficult to know what it would mean for him to feel inspired and to think of it as service to God. If Sallie does her job well, it may lead to results she finds morally repugnant. It is tempting to think that Ben and Mary need to care *less* passionately about their jobs and find some time in their lives for other things. Others in the congregation are retired or out of work. What would it mean to tell them that being called by God to a job can give our lives meaning? Does that leave them with meaningless lives?

Most theologians and ethicists have given these problems little attention. A variety of church pronouncements on work — papal encyclicals, statements by the World Council of Churches, and a recent Presbyterian document on vocation — tend mostly to address employers, government officials, or voters, reminding them that they need to help give workers a better economic situation and more humane working conditions. Such advice is all to the good, but it offers me little help in knowing how *I* as a Christian ought to think about *my* job.

Part of the answer, I suspect, is that in our complex society there can be no one answer regarding how to think as a Christian about one's job. Christian churches include people with different sorts of jobs and different relations to them: day laborers, professionals, househusbands or housewives, one-career families, two-career families, single parents, the retired, the unemployed, people putting in their time till retirement, workaholics. No single message about work and Christian life fits them all.

That diversity is nothing new. Luther preached to both kings and peasants, and surely an honest preacher would have said different things to them about their jobs. In some respects, though, the problems have grown more complex in the in-

tervening centuries. Even long after the Reformation, most
workers were either farmers or craftsmen. Farmers can think
about stewardship of the land, passing on fertile topsoil or
healthy fruit trees to future generations. Someone making a
table or a wedding dress by hand can think about the beauty
and excellence of the product as a personal accomplishment, a
matter of pride. For many office workers or people on an assembly line, those categories no longer seem to apply. Moreover,
many traditional forms of the doctrine of vocation assumed that
men had jobs as their vocation, while women were called to
care for home and children.

Thus, if we are still to think of our jobs as callings in which
we serve God, we need to redefine how we understand vocation. We could begin with two principles basic to Christian
faith. First, our *ultimate* calling is to glorify God. Second, we
serve God in our callings, not to earn salvation, but in gratitude
for grace already received. Those general principles make a difference in how we think about practical questions concerning
our jobs.

Our chief end, the famous opening of the Westminster
Shorter Catechism declares, "is to glorify God, and to enjoy
him forever." The glorification of God is our ultimate end. But
what does that mean? In *A River Runs through It*, Norman
Maclean tells how in his family, where "there was no clear
line between religion and fly fishing," his father, a Presbyterian
pastor out in Montana, used to teach Norman and his brother
Paul the catechism. They rarely got beyond the first answer:
" 'Man's chief end is to glorify God, and to enjoy Him forever.'
This always seems to satisfy him, as indeed such a beautiful
answer should have." Years later, Norman and his father think
about Paul's troubled life — full of too much drinking and too
much fighting — which was ended far too soon after his being
beaten to death by the butt of a revolver in an alley. They agree
about two things — Paul was a great fly fisherman, and he was
beautiful. Whatever other failures in his life, he did something
superbly well, and in that, as a creature of God exercising to
the full the excellences given him, he was glorifying the God
who made him and gave him those excellences.

Chariots of Fire tells the story of Eric Liddell, the Scottish evangelical Christian who ran in the 1924 Olympics. At one point in the film, his sister urges him to give up the frivolity of running to devote himself exclusively to preparation for mission work, but he protests, "God...made me fast, and when I run I feel His pleasure. To give it up would be to hold him in contempt.... To win is to honor him." When we do something well, the doing of it can be a form of the praise of God — whether by a gifted athlete, an artist, a carpenter at work on a house, or a shoe repairer making old shoes good as new.

The great Swiss theologian Karl Barth tells how one Saturday night he went to a variety show where every laugh line was perfectly timed, all the performers at the peak of their crafts. Next morning, he heard an ill-prepared and badly presented sermon. "Could I resist the impression," he asks,

> that, formally at least, the right thing had been done at the place of very secular amusement and not at the place where the Gospel is preached and worship offered.... Whatever our work or its particular purpose, we are either heart and soul in a thing or we take things easily.... God knows perfectly well whether we are heart and soul in a matter, or whether we are merely playing at it.

When we do our work with our heart and soul in it, we can glorify God. Perhaps the world will little honor us. No matter. Some jobs with little prestige accomplish obviously important social goods. Better, Barth says, to be a good sewer cleaner than a bad theologian! But even when the social good is less clear, there is still the beauty of a task well done. One thinks of the medieval tale of the juggler who, wishing to honor the Virgin Mary, did the only thing he could do well; he juggled — not as useful as cleaning a sewer, to be sure, but, if done well and in the right spirit, the exercise to the full of a gift given by God.

Sometimes, then, we really can glorify God by doing our jobs well. But it is the glorification of God that is the ultimate goal; the job is not an end in itself. And sometimes we glorify God best by refusing to do a job. Christians will do a day's work for a day's pay. We will witness to our integrity and honor by doing what we contracted to do when we took the job, hard work when it is called for. We will not be whiners or slackers, lest our failings bring disrepute on our faith. But we have loyalties more important than those to job or employer — our loyalties to God — and sometimes they will have to take precedence.

If the job calls for something dishonest, we will be at best reluctant and unhappy workers. At the extreme, we may even refuse or quit. And we will not interpret *dishonesty* too narrowly. When the Ten Commandments forbid stealing, John Calvin wrote, they do not prohibit only "brigandage" and "fraud" but also "a more concealed craftiness, when someone's goods are snatched from them by seemingly legal means." "The intricate deceptions with which a crafty person sets out to snare one of simpler mind," he continued, may "elude human judgment," but God recognizes them as theft. A good many jobs these days involve snaring people of simpler mind, one way or another. Christians ought to resist doing jobs like that.

Such resistance can lead to tough consequences. One can get stuck in a professional dead end or even lose a job, and sometimes such choices face people for whom another job may not be easy to come by. Sometimes, though, what hurts most is not the economic consequence but the frustration: "I could have been really good at that job, a great success, if only my stupid moral principles hadn't gotten in the way." If doing the job was an end in itself, then this is irremediable tragedy. But, if the point of doing the job well was to glorify God by using one's gifts, then maybe that person glorifies God best in refusing to do a job that he or she thinks is wrong. In that sense, the person stuck in a professional dead end or even out of a job because of principles may be beautiful to God's glory.

Sometimes, though, the problem is not that a job calls for something wicked — merely that it does not seem to offer much room for excellence. The job is routine; the rules are constricting; the boss is a petty tyrant. In this case, maybe the good of the job lies elsewhere. To take the most obvious case, perhaps it provides the money to support the worker and his or her family. It is interesting that when Paul talked about the jobs he had held — he was a tentmaker by trade — he emphasized that he thereby earned his own keep and was not a financial burden to anyone (see 2 Thess. 3:8; 1 Cor. 4:12; 9:6; 2 Cor. 11:7). As long as the job is honest work, there is nothing to be ashamed of in holding a job — any sort of job — principally because one needs the money. Maybe a person's calling lies not so much in doing the job but in supporting a family or in just preserving a sense of self-reliance in difficult circumstances. Maybe that is the way some people glorify God.

In contrast, some will find their principal calling in a job that pays no money at all — in volunteer work for the community or the church. A paying job takes care of the bills, but things done on weekends or in the evening provide the real sense of meaning and fulfillment of God's purpose in one's life.

Sometimes, to take another case, it will be relations with co-workers rather than the job itself that provide one's calling in the workplace. In every factory or office there are those who offer to help someone who is having trouble, who seek out the lonely or depressed for a conversation, who ask about an ailing parent or a child in trouble, who protest when racism or sexism demeans someone. Christians ought to be such people, and the doing of such good deeds may for some be their central calling. Sometimes the friendly server in a restaurant or the mail carrier who gives a cheerful greeting may provide the only positive human contact in a customer's life. Is their job a calling? Perhaps not so much the job itself as the opportunity it provides for the witness of their faith and the glorifying of God in their everyday acts of kindness.

Such various forms of witnessing on the job can give the world of work importance even for those whose actual job leaves them with little sense of fulfillment. For others, however, as I have already suggested, problems arise because their jobs can seem *so* worth doing as to leave little time for anything else. If I am a police investigator tracking down criminals or a teacher making a crucial difference in students' lives or a lawyer defending an unjustly accused client or a skilled nurse or surgeon, then it rightly seems as if the work I do really matters, and the more time and energy I devote to it, the better. In such jobs, I would have no trouble thinking of my work as my vocation.

We have learned, of course, to speak dismissively of workaholics, as if too much commitment to one's job were a form of addiction. Sometimes, spending endless time and energy at work *can* be a way of hiding from other problems. But sometimes the job is so much worth doing that the sense that I am doing more good the more time I give is — within the limits imposed by health and sanity — simply true. In such cases, is the more I do the better? Here too, there is no single answer for all Christians. Some of us, for parts of our lives, may have the calling to live a life utterly wrapped up in a rewarding and meaningful job. That may not be compatible with being a spouse or a parent. It may involve limits in our roles as active participants in our congregations. But such a life should not serve as *the* model of what it is like to have a vocation, as if anything else fell disappointingly short.

Most Christians are called to balance many competing demands in their lives. Luther himself admitted that any one individual has a number of different stations and therefore will have more than one vocation. Even when my job is rewarding, something I can do well and serves the good, I have other obligations. I am a child of parents, a spouse, a parent of children, a citizen of a nation, an inhabitant of a neighborhood, a member of a Christian congregation. I am a person in my own right too, with a love of music, skill as an amateur photographer, interest in watching the stars at night, and I would be less myself, the particular creature God created, if I did nothing to develop these interests.

Yet all these legitimate demands can make me feel as if they are pulling me in a dozen directions. On a practical level, Christians ought to support efforts to reduce such tensions — good day care on the job or viable part-time options for women and men who want to give more time to parenting without sacrificing their careers. But such helps do not solve the problem. Indeed, there is often no magic solution to such tensions. Christians struggling with such issues can remember that none of their particular callings — to job, to parenting, to anything else — is their ultimate purpose in life, which lies in glorifying God and therefore in developing all the facets of the persons they were created to be. Even when we think that God has called us to our jobs, we must not let the job become the only point of our lives.

When we realize that we may have to balance competing ways of serving God in our lives, that makes things more complicated. In the face of such complexity, it can be particularly important to remember the second principle I mentioned earlier — we serve God in our callings, not to earn salvation, but in gratitude for grace already received. *Grace* just means "unmerited love," and Christian teaching about grace reminds us that we do not try to be good — in our jobs or elsewhere — so that God will love us, and therefore we will be saved. God loves us anyway, and we could never be good enough to earn salvation: "God proves his love for us in that while we still were sinners Christ died for us" (Rom. 5:8). Whatever we do in the service of God, we do it in praise and gratitude for a love already received. "To trust in works," Luther once wrote, "is equivalent to giving oneself the honor and taking it from God." It is God's grace that saves us.

Should we therefore, as Paul already imagined skeptics asking, "sin the more that grace may abound the more"? As Paul replied, "By no means!" (Rom. 6:1–2). If we receive such astonishing love from God, we will want eagerly to respond in gratitude. Indeed, freed of worrying about our salvation, we will be able to praise God and serve our fellow humans without ulterior motives. No need to think about keeping score in how well we are deserving to be saved: we help others simply because they need help and worship God simply because God deserves worship.

Thinking about everything we do under the category of gratitude frees us in all sorts of ways. Calvin wrote of the matter eloquently (he here compares God to a father, though he elsewhere said that it was just as appropriate to think of God as like a mother, and the point is the contrast of loving parent with stern master):

> Those who are bound by the yoke of the law are like servants on whom their masters impose certain tasks each day. Unless the exact measure of their tasks is met, they think they have achieved nothing and dare not face their masters. But children, who are dealt with more generously and more liberally by their fathers, do not hesitate to show them unfinished projects that they have only begun, or even spoiled a little. Even if they have not succeeded in doing quite what they wanted, they are confident that their obedience and readiness of mind will be accepted. Such children we ought to be, trusting con-

fidently that our most lenient father will approve of them, however small, rough, or imperfect they may be.

If we think about our work in such a context of grace, then a good many problems begin to solve themselves.

If we are in a position where we have the opportunity to use some gift or skill we possess to help others or simply to manifest the excellence that God has given us, then of course we will want to do so. How would we not thus seek to show our gratitude to the God who gave us all that we have and are? On the other hand, if we are hit with bad luck and do not have the circumstances in which to do much useful work, then we particularly need to remember that we were not in any event earning our salvation. Perhaps illness or severe handicap prevents me from holding down a job. Perhaps the economy has turned sour, and there simply seems no market for the skills I possess. *My* calling may be simply to show patience under affliction. The great poet John Milton was struck blind early in life. He angrily wondered how God could expect him to write his greatest poetry to God's glory with such a handicap. But then he realized that God did not need his poetry:

> "Doth God exact day-labor, light denied?"
> I fondly ask; but Patience to prevent
> That murmur soon replies, "God doth not need
> Either man's works or his own gifts."

God rejoices when we use the abilities we have been given to the full in God's praise. But God does not need what we might have done if only we had not been limited by circumstances. God does not need anything from us, and God is not keeping score.

Here too it is important to resist generalizations. I *may* find a richly fulfilling job in spite of a severe handicap — one thinks at the extreme of Stephen Hawking's extraordinary career as a physicist. I *may* think of some way, in the midst of a bad economy, to turn my abilities to creative and unexpected use — whether in imaginatively finding a new sort of job or in finding productive ways to serve my church and community while I am job hunting. But sometimes not. My value as a human being before God does not depend on such things. God has already loved me with more love than I can imagine; God does not need my accomplishments.

Alternatively, I may find that I have more opportunities than I know how to handle. My job is richly rewarding, and there seems no end to the time I could profitably devote to it. I also covet every minute I can spend with my spouse and my children. People want me to run for school board next year, and it seems as if I could make a real difference. But there are just not enough hours in the day. "I was never tempted," the seventeenth-century Puritan Richard Baxter once complained, "so much to grudge at God's natural ordering of man, in any thing, as that we are fated to waste so much of our little time in sleep...that it deprived me of so much precious time, which else might have been used in some profitable work." Baxter has uncounted descendants in every competitive profession.

But Baxter misunderstood grace. We ought not to be fretting that we do not have enough waking hours to do God's work. To quote Karl Barth again,

> By our outward and inward work we can and should confirm [God's work] in all seriousness and with all our might, but we can do so bravely and cheerfully because it is *God's* work which we are summoned to confirm, and we are thus relieved entirely from the task of achieving or even supplementing this basic affirmation by our own work.... We have neither to repeat, emulate, nor augment this work of God. We have simply to attest it.... We have simply to praise God with our activity.... We should do our work with diligence but also with the recollection that God is Lord, Master, Provider, Warrior, Victor, Author and Finisher, and therefore with the relief and relaxation which spring from this recognition.

In understandable reaction against the images of a stern, powerful God, much contemporary theology has talked of our cooperation with God. We are, so the argument goes, cocreators of the world and therefore responsible and of ultimate significance. It is a way of valuing our activity, but the danger is that such talk puts the burden back on us and loses that wonderful sense that we are free *because* God is in control, and we can take the risks of imaginative expression of our gratitude for what God has given us.

Though there is often a single right answer as to how to earn a reward, there is rarely a single right way to express gratitude. When something wonderful has been done for us, there are often many different things we could, with equal appropriateness, do in return. If we start worrying overmuch about having done one thing and thereby failed to do another, we are failing to understand either generosity or gratitude. In a way, it is difficult to go wrong: God recognizes gratitude in whatever form. "Like good stewards of the manifold grace of God," then we should "serve one another with whatever grace each of you has received" (1 Pet. 4:10).

If we return to the four opening cases — Mary and Ben, the committed physicians; Dan, working at a frustrating job to support his family; Sallie, faced with a choice between compromising her moral principles or maybe losing her job — what have we learned? We have not found any simple solutions. No one "proper Christian attitude" toward one's job fits every case. No neat formula solves any of the problems. Theology should not make genuinely hard questions seem easy. Still, if we keep in mind that our primary vocation is to glorify God and that we do so in gratitude for grace already received, and not to earn salvation, then we may at least avoid some kinds of mistakes.

If we have been blessed with many wonderful opportunities, then we ought to feel them as blessings, not as burdens. We glorify God in using God's gifts to do something excellently. But we express gratitude to God whichever gifts we use. Common sense may sometimes indicate priorities and balances, but God is not keeping score, angry and ready to punish if we do not make use of each and every blessing to the full. In the confidence of God's grace, we really can learn to relax a little.

Conversely, if we find ourselves without the opportunity for a particularly fulfilling job or even forced to take a step back in our career for the sake of our moral principles, we are not thereby failing. Perhaps our calling, our way of witnessing to our faith, is to take a moral stand or to stick with a job for the sake of our love of our families or to help people in the workplace or to find our real fulfillment in another aspect of our lives. We can glorify God in so many different ways.

In her moving book *Also a Mother*, Bonnie Miller-McLemore has written of the tensions that have particularly burdened women in sorting out the balances between parenting and career. Too often, she says, a work ethic that emphasizes vocation "has ended...by providing a piety and cultural context that condones self-righteous individual achievement, selfish self-sufficiency, and ruthless ambition." After all, Christians have sometimes said, "If this is what God has called me to do, then everyone and everything else had best get out of the way." But such an understanding of vocation makes a particular job, rather than our glorification of God, our primary calling and loses sight of the reassuring, relaxing, good news of grace.

For Further Reading

Barth, Karl. *Church Dogmatics,* vol. 3, pt. 4, pp. 470–565. Trans. A. T. Mackay et al. Edinburgh: T. & T. Clark, 1961. Offers, as Barth always does, rich reflections.

Miller-McLemore, Bonnie F. *Also a Mother: Work and Family as Theological Dilemma.* Nashville: Abingdon, 1994. Contains the most thoughtful feminist discussion of the topic.

Volf, Miroslav. *Work in the Spirit: Toward a Theology of Work.* New York: Oxford University Press, 1991. The only full-scale recent treatment of the topic.

10

MUST CHRISTIANS BELIEVE IN HELL?

George Hunsinger

Four distinct perspectives on hell have been evident in the Christian tradition. Although in steady decline since the seventeenth century, the belief that the damned are punished with eternal torment still remains the official teaching for most of Christendom, with a history of vigorous support that continues to the present day. Not having gained clear ascendancy, however, until perhaps about the fourth century, the idea of eternal punishment has never lacked alternatives and principled opposition. In both ancient and modern times, doctrines known as *universalism, annihilationism,* and *reverent agnosticism* have attracted important advocates. All four views will be surveyed and briefly assessed here.

Eternal Punishment: The Catholic Faith

No one has had a stronger influence on Christian beliefs about hell than Augustine (354–430), the bishop of Hippo and great theologian of the church. The lines of biblical interpretation and rational argument that he developed have formed the basis of the catholic faith on this topic ever since he set them forth. Views such as those he championed made their way into the so-called Athanasian Creed (ca. 381–428), which proclaimed that at the conclusion of the last judgment, "those who have done evil will go into everlasting fire." Essentially the same

A longer version of this essay is forthcoming in the *Scottish Journal of Theology* under the title "Hellfire and Damnation: Four Ancient and Modern Views."

position was adopted at the Fourth Lateran Council in 1215: those who are damned "will receive a perpetual punishment with the devil." This belief has been normative not only for the Roman Catholic Church but also for the confessional standards of the Protestant Reformation as instructed by Luther and Calvin. Today the contours of Augustine's position appear essentially unchanged in the arguments of Roman Catholics like Cardinal Joseph Ratzinger and conservative-evangelical Protestants like J. I. Packer. Modified versions of the Augustinian view are also present in contemporary discussion.

The definition that Augustine gave to the doctrine of hell can be analyzed into seven basic components. Although many of these components were of course present in Christian belief prior to his time, Augustine systematized and defended them in an unprecedented way. The result was what we may call "the strong view of hell." Analyzing this view will provide us with a useful yardstick against which alternative or competing views within the Christian tradition can be measured and understood. The seven components of the strong, Augustinian view are as follows.

First, hell is actual. Not all human beings are saved, and those who aren't are consigned to eternal damnation. Hell, as Augustine understood it, is no mere theoretical possibility. It is the eternal destiny that awaits the majority of the human race.

Second, hell is severe. No greater torment can be suffered than the anguish of hell, for it involves the loss of God, the true source of life and happiness for which we were created. The torment of the lost is thus the worst of all evils.

Third, hell is endless. Those who suffer it never perish, and their torment affords no escape. Because they are not permitted to die, it can be said that for them death itself never dies. It is a torment in which those who endure it will be dying for all eternity.

Fourth, hell is penal. It is the penalty for sin as appointed by God. Since the remedy for sin is faith in Jesus Christ, hell is the penalty for those who lack this faith. It is undoubtedly a form of retribution rather than a form of remedy. It is not meant to lead to repentance or amendment of life because the time for repentance has passed.

Fifth, hell is just. It is the punishment that corresponds to the offense. No other punishment would be adequate to match the wickedness of sin against God. Who would think otherwise, Augustine asked, but a fool? Being the very standard of justice, God could not possibly do something unjust. God simply inflicts the punishment on the wicked that they deserve.

Sixth, hell is ordained by God. It is not merely an impersonal consequence of sin, nor is it merely something that sinners suffer as a consequence of misusing their freedom. God consigns sinners to eternal fire by denying them eternal salvation. If God chooses to convert evil persons, he demonstrates his mercy. If he chooses not to do so, he demonstrates his justice. No one is saved unless God wills it; and if God wills it, it must necessarily be accomplished. Conversely, no one is damned unless God so wills it according to his perfect justice.

Finally, hell is inscrutable. The inner logic of God's dealings with sinful human beings is beyond our capacity to fathom. How it can be fair for God to save some but not others when all are equally sinful is inscrutable. How the severity of endless torment throughout all eternity is commensurate with the actual offense of sin is also beyond our ken. Our only recourse in such matters is to defer to the greater wisdom of God.

As noted, this articulation of the catholic faith has remained definitive to the present day. In that light, two more points are worthy of note. In the first place, in its understanding of the New Testament witness, the Augustinian tradition always assigns pride of place to Matthew 25:31–46, the passage in which the Son of man returns in glory for the last judgment. All the nations gather before him to be separated into the sheep at his right hand and the goats at his left. The former depart to eternal life and the latter to eternal punishment. The perfect parallelism of the two destinies — both being described as "eternal" in apparently the same sense — presents a difficult crux of interpretation for any biblically based view that would reject the Augustinian tradition. Whether the passage from Matthew 25 really deserves the hermeneutical primacy that has been assigned to it, however, remains a matter of dispute.

In the second place, modern exponents of the received tradition often deviate from Augustine at a crucial point. Their apologies for hell typically turn on an appeal to human freedom. At least since the nineteenth century, a systematic effort can be detected to discharge God from responsibility for eternal punishment. In other words, modern interpreters (including official or quasi-official theologians like Ratzinger and Packer) typically adopt a strategy that places them significantly at variance with two of Augustine's main points: hell as divinely ordained and hell as inscrutable. In modern apologetics hell is supposed to seem less inscrutable when human responsibility assumes the spotlight while divine judgment withdraws quietly to the shadows. Divine sovereignty is thus displaced by an emphasis on human "freedom," and the frailty of human understanding is eclipsed by claims to "intelligibility." Rarely do Augustine's modern heirs pause to ask themselves whether the gains of this strategy really outweigh the losses or, indeed, whether the strategy really works at all.

Universal Salvation: The Minority Report

If the official faith has its champion in Augustine, the best-known unauthorized alternative finds its ancient defender in Origen (ca. 185–254), the brilliant Alexandrian thinker who has been described (though not quite aptly) as the first "systematic theologian" in the history of the church. Origen developed a kind of "Christian Platonism" that sometimes seems more Platonist than Christian, and this mixed outlook displays itself nicely in his arguments for universal salvation. His views, of course, did not always find a welcome reception. *Apokatastasis*, or the final restoration of all things — an idea associated with Origen's name — was explicitly condemned by a council at Constantinople in 543 and possibly also by the Fifth Ecumenical Council (553). Nevertheless, if we take Augustine's view and compare it with Origen's, we obtain the following results. Origen and Augustine agree that hell is actual and just, but Origen denies that it is endless. This disagreement then modifies the other four points. The Origenist hell is less severe than the Augustinian. It is penal but not in the same sense. Although divinely ordained, it allots greater scope than Augustine did to human freedom. And it is finally less inscrutable than the Augustinian version would require.

For Origen as for Augustine, hell is actual. Everyone must indeed pass through divine judgment as through a purifying fire. That fire is God himself, who consumes human sins, crushing, devouring, and purging them. The process is undoubtedly severe — consisting, Origen acknowledged, of torments, penalty, and torture for the soul. Yet its ultimate purpose is not retributive, as in Augustine, but remedial. It is a form of very bitter medicine. God is a physician who requires drastic remedies in restoring the soul to health. His wrath toward the sinner is not vindictive but corrective. God does not inflict punishment except as the means that purifies the soul through unavoidable torment.

Remedial punishment clearly implies that the torment will not last forever and that all human beings will finally be saved. God's punishment is not everlasting. All things will finally be restored to one great end, which according to Origen is like the beginning. God never ceases his work of salvation until all resistance to his will is overcome.

In his account of salvation, Origen has to address the perennial question of how divine grace and human freedom are related. He does not assign the same kind of unconditional sovereignty to divine grace as we found in Augustine. Although Origen clearly sees grace as indispensable, he also views it as dependent upon the work of human striving, even when grace is finally decisive. At one point he imagines a sailing ship that is navigated by sailors and driven by the wind. The navigation is like human freedom while the wind is like divine grace. Each "cooperates" with the other. If we use our freedom properly and well, God will always assist us with benevolence. If we do not use it well, however, a contest exists between freedom and grace until the former finally yields to the latter.

The end of all things, as Origen conceived it, involves a return to the perfect harmony of the beginning. This metaphysical return seems more nearly Platonic than Christian in inspiration. It assumes a difficult scheme of preexistent souls acquiring earthly bodies only as a result of the fall into sin and then living in various states of disorder and disarray until finally rescued through trials of purgation and grace after death. It is not always easy to determine how much influence the great metaphysical parabola of descent and ascent is exercising on Origen's thoughts.

This Platonic scheme is perhaps in the background of Origen's allegorizing exegesis of Scripture, which allows him to read New Testament passages about eternal punishment in a much freer way than did Augustine, who worked so unflinchingly with the literal sense. Allegorizing exegesis and metaphysical scheme, however, do not fully explain what is perhaps finally Origen's most salient difference from Augustine on the question of eternal damnation: his granting of unqualified primacy to the benevolence and mercy of God. Though Origen's God is not without his own inscrutability, it is not the inscrutability of an apparently malignant caprice.

What is at stake between the Augustinian and Origenist traditions taken at their best, one might say, are two different views about how to interpret Scripture. The Augustinians hug close to the shoreline, it would seem, whereas the Origenists launch much further out to sea. The Augustinians accuse the universalists of overlooking too much prominent timber when sighting the mainland, whereas the Origenists accuse the retributionists of not seeing the forest for the trees. The Augustinians would say that the forest is fraught with inscrutability; the Origenists, that any inscrutability is overridden by intelligible significance. The Augustinians would point to the rank undergrowth of sin in its great obduracy and abomination; the Origenists, to the towering peaks of divine love. The Augustinians would insist that faith must arise in this life as the necessary condition of deliverance; the Origenists would retort that the sufficient condition of deliverance is found in the assured persistence of divine grace. The debate, taken as a whole, might arguably seem to result in an impasse. Whether the impasse can perhaps be resolved is the theme to which we now turn.

Annihilationism: Retribution Tempered by Clemency

One effort to resolve the impasse is called *annihilationism*. This proposal is perhaps best understood as a cautious modification of the traditional Augustinian view. It agrees with the official tradition on every point but one. Hell is affirmed as actual, severe, penal, just, divinely ordained, and inscrutable, but it is not affirmed as endless. Like the Origenist tradition, this proposal suggests instead that the punishment of hell is of limited duration. Unlike the Origenist tradition, however, the punishment is limited not by restoration but by annihilation. The wicked do not suffer eternal torment in the sense of suffering for all eternity after they are condemned. They are simply judged, terrified, and destroyed. Although this idea is not lacking in severity, its severity is tempered by clemency. It is thus less inscrutable than the Augustinian view regarding how eternal punishment can be compatible with the nature of the divine compassion.

No distinguished theologian seems to have defended this proposal in the early church. Its only known proponent was Arnobius (fl. 304–310), an apologist who wrote a treatise attacking the errors of pagan worship and mythology. However, although lacking in distinguished defenders, annihilationism did have distinguished opponents. Both Tertullian and Augustine were familiar with the idea, and both put some effort into refuting it. It seems unlikely that they would have done so if there had not been at least some dissatisfaction among the Christian rank and file regarding the severity of the received tradition.

Annihilationism has reappeared in recent times with some especially noteworthy defenders in the evangelical wing of the Protestant church. Prominent evangelicals like F. F. Bruce, Philip Hughes, John Wenham, and John Stott have all endorsed such a view. The arguments of these proponents, as was the case with Augustine, are typically marked by careful attention to the literal sense of the biblical texts before any generalizations are ventured about the nature of God. An attempt is thus made to modify the traditional view on the basis of the very same texts by which it has always been defended.

A vigorous and concise case for annihilationism has been published by John Stott (b. 1921), the prolific Christian writer, evangelical elder statesman, and former rector of the All Souls Anglican Church in London. Stott defines hell as a banishment from God that is real, terrible, and irreversible. Against the Origenist tradition, he sees no hint in the New Testament that a later reprieve or amnesty is possible. The point he wishes to explore is whether hell will involve, as the Augustinian tradition claims, the experience of endless suffering.

Stott considers and interprets the relevant New Testament passages to mean that the impenitent finally perish. Those passages, notes Stott, typically speak of destruction rather than of everlasting conscious torment, and the prominent imagery of fire can be interpreted as the means by which the impenitent are annihilated. More broadly, Stott remarks that the idea of eternal conscious torment does not seem compatible with the biblical revelation of God's justice. Although the immense gravity of sin is not to be minimized, the punishment of eternal torment does not seem proportionate to the offense. Stott in effect rejects the Augustinian appeal to inscrutability at this point. Finally, he reckons with important passages in the New Testament about the universal reign of God. While they do not mean that all persons will be saved — here Stott is firmly within the bounds of the Augustinian tradition — they are easier to understand if hell means final destruction and the impenitent will have ceased to exist.

Perhaps the strangest thing about Stott's arguments, which are not weak as far as they go, is that they don't really go very far. They finally seem to be more nearly biblicist than evangelical in character. Jesus as Teacher is afforded more prominence than Jesus as Savior. Divine justice is considered from the standpoint of fairness, but not from the more deeply evangelical standpoint that would ask about how God's justice is integrated with God's mercy. By his own admission Stott cherishes the hope that most human beings will be saved. Although this seems a hope well worth cherishing, he offers no real basis to make it convincing.

Reverent Agnosticism: None of the Above

Although Karl Barth (1886–1968) is often labeled as a *universalist*, he is best understood as standing in the tradition of "holy silence." Found especially in the ancient Greek fathers, though never widespread, this interpretive tradition may claim Clement of Alexandria (ca. 160–215), Gregory of Nyssa (ca. 331–395), and Maximus the Confessor (580–662) as among its representatives. Unable to resolve the tensions in the New Testament, it is a tradition that opts finally for silence.

Barth picks up and renews this neglected approach. If a forced option is urged between the proposition "All are saved" and the counterproposition "Not all are saved," his answer in effect is "None of the above." Barth deliberately leaves the question open, though not in a neutral fashion but with a strong tilt toward universal hope. Like Origen he finds it difficult to see how God will not fully triumph in grace at the end. But like Augustine he has a chastened sense that human sin is profoundly inscrutable. More like Origen than Augustine, he does not find a fully clear picture emerging from Scripture. But more like Augustine than Origen, his final concern as a theologian is to honor the sovereign freedom of grace. The result is holy silence or, as it has sometimes also been called, *reverent agnosticism.*

Barth is explicit in his rejection of the Origenist doctrine of *apokatastasis.* In its typical form, Barth observes, this doctrine argues for the restoration of all things on the basis of two optimistic postulates: that God is infinitely patient and that human freedom will inevitably yield at last to divine grace. Not only are these postulates improper, as Barth sees it, but the whole line of argument is really a groundless abstraction. The reasoning is abstract because it works with arbitrary principles rather than divine revelation as attested in Holy Scripture. When understood concretely, it is clear that God does not owe eternal patience to human beings who persist in the depravity of their sin, nor does God owe them final deliverance. Sinners, according to biblical revelation, stand constantly under the threat of divine judgment and condemnation.

When sin is viewed concretely, moreover, it is clear that human freedom cannot be taken for granted as something that we just have. Freedom in the only relevant sense is at once the gift and requirement of God, and human beings have it only as they receive it and exercise it in obedience to God and by complete reliance on his grace. Freedom is not something that God merely "respects" in us, for it is not clear just what kind of freedom we possess to be respected, unless it is the "freedom" to continue sinning. On the question of grace and freedom, Barth stands in the Pauline tradition as developed by Augustine and radicalized by Luther in works like *The Bondage of the Will.* Perhaps the main characteristic of this tradition is that it heightens rather than resolves the conceptual tensions between divine sovereignty and human responsibility. These tensions can arguably not be resolved without distorting the actual encounters and renewed decisions at stake in the ongoing divine/human relationship that is situated in a living history.

If universal salvation should actually occur, writes Barth, it can only be as the unexpected work of grace. It is not something we can calculate by a process of abstract reasoning that forgets that God is still God and that human beings are still sinners. Not even the cross and resurrection of Jesus Christ can be used as the basis for such abstract calculations. Although theological consistency might seem to require a stance of universalism, it is not for fallen sinners to deduce what God "must" do in consummating his work of salvation.

However, although there can be a danger of saying too much, there can also be a danger, Barth believes, of saying too little. The need for "holy silence" does not remove the need for "holy speech." Although universal salvation cannot be deduced as a necessity, it cannot be excluded as a possibility. Neither the logical deduction nor the definite exclusion would properly respect the concrete freedom of God. When the reality of Jesus Christ is taken properly into account, it does point, Barth affirms, in the direction of an eternal divine patience and therefore of universal salvation. This salvation would be supremely the work of God. Although as sinners we have no claim upon it, we are commanded to hope and pray for it. Cautiously and yet distinctly, we are to hope and pray that God's compassion will not fail and that he will not cast us off forever.

No one, Barth teaches, will escape the wrath and judgment of God: "For we must all appear before the judgment seat of Christ" (2 Cor. 5:10). In this judgment God does not pay obeisance to our freedom. On the contrary, he takes our freedom from us. He makes us so powerless that he hands us over to the power of our enemy, a power that is too great for us, that it may dominate us. This enemy into whose hands we are delivered is our own sinful work. In judgment God abandons us to this work and therefore to our actual destruction.

We do not withstand this judgment. We fall, but we fall only where we have put ourselves. We are not made alive; we are slain. This is the work of the wrath of God. It is a harsh, burning, and destructive wrath. If the New Testament is to be taken seriously, the severity of divine judgment may not be softened or diminished in any way. Although the context for these remarks shows that Barth is thinking directly of those who have fallen away from their faith, or of those who have rejected their election, there is no reason to believe that he is not thinking indirectly of all others as well. For there is a solidarity in sin that will have similar dreadful consequences in punishment for all, regardless of any differences of degree or of election or of faith.

The only question is not whether we will be judged according to our works but whether there is somehow hope beyond judgment. Is there a possibility in and with our being finally destroyed that God may somehow still be enjoined to be our God? Is there hope beyond hope, beyond the completed judgment, beyond our annihilation as sinners? There is still the prospect of it, suggests Barth, even if only at the vanishing point. God's wrath is not an end in itself. Something beyond destruction still remains. The eschatological possibility still exists for salvation on the day of the Lord. The eternal fire of punishment is not removed or weakened but is boundless in itself, yet in this boundlessness it is still enclosed by a limit. Note that Barth does not separate retributive and remedial elements in the final punishment, nor does he diminish its severity. He looks only for a larger and hidden divine Yes that may yet surround, limit, and enclose the necessary No in all its terrible severity.

If God's mercy were proclaimed without judgment or if God's love were proclaimed without wrath or if false comfort were proclaimed in which none were slain to be made alive and none were alive who had not first been slain, then the cross of Christ would be unintelligible. God imposes no severity on others that, in the death of his Son on the cross, he has not already suffered himself to an incalculably greater degree. The punishment that we may suffer, writes Barth, is immediately overshadowed and surpassed by that which Jesus Christ had to endure for the sake of our sins. Because of what he endured, however, there is not only a universal solidarity in sin but also and all the more a universal solidarity in grace, though we do not know in just what sense God will finally choose to carry the latter through for those who failed to come to faith in this life.

The only certain triumph of hell that we know, states Barth, is the cross of Golgotha on which Jesus died for our sins. He suffered what he suffered so that no one would need ever to suffer it again. We are told of only one person who has suffered hell in this way. That person is Jesus Christ. Because he was lost and was found again, no one need ever be lost apart from him. When we know this person by faith and remember what he endured for the sake of the world, then no matter how desperate the situation may be, we will not abandon hope for anyone, not even for ourselves.

Conclusion

The strong view of hell as represented by Augustine would seem to be admirable at least for its unflinching consistency and for its steadfast appeal to the primacy and sovereignty of divine grace. If there is ever to be any larger hope within the bounds of traditional belief beyond the state of the question as Augustine left it, then that hope would seem necessarily to rest not on an appeal to autonomous human freedom (as in the weaker modern apologies) but rather on an appeal to sovereign grace. For if it is indeed grace and grace alone, as Augustine argued, that separates the saved from the lost and if it is true, as he also urged, that God can change the evil wills of human beings whenever he chooses and can direct them to salvation, then the church may truly have grounds for a larger hope than Augustine found it possible to affirm. The New Testament texts as Augustine read them would have to be reconfigured into a very different hermeneutical whole.

Although that whole may have been glimpsed by Origen, the hermeneutical tradition that he spawned has too often been encumbered by rationalizing and otherwise extraneous considerations. At its best, however, that tradition has focused concretely on the cross of Christ as the demonstration of God's love for the entire world. On that basis it has refused to separate God's justice so drastically from God's mercy, or indeed to leave the two standing in apparent, severe, and inscrutable contradiction. It has also refused to allow the important universalist passages in the New Testament to be so thoroughly marginalized by those that depict the ultimate consequences of divine wrath. If the mark of a good theology is that it knows how to honor the necessary mysteries, then there may be higher and reconfigured mysteries that the Augustinian tradition knows not of.

For Further Reading

Barth, Karl. *Church Dogmatics,* vol. 2, pt. 2, pp. 458–505, esp. pp. 477–87. Edinburgh: T. & T. Clark, 1957.

Barth, Karl. *Church Dogmatics,* vol. 4, pt. 3, Second Half, pp. 902–42, esp. pp. 918, 931–32. Edinburgh: T. & T. Clark, 1962.

Norris, Frederick W. "Universal Salvation in Origen and Maximus," in *Universalism and the Doctrine of Hell.* ed. Nigel M. de S. Cameron. Grand Rapids: Baker Book House, 1992. Origen's views are scattered throughout his extant writings. An excellent anthology of interest to the theme.

Stott, John R. *Evangelical Essentials: A Liberal-Evangelical Dialogue* (Downers Grove, Ill.: InterVarsity, 1988. Stott's case for annihilationism.

Walker, D. P. *The Decline of Hell.* London: Routledge & Kegan Paul, 1964. The fate of the traditional Augustinian belief since the seventeenth century. Augustine's views are found most conveniently in his *Enchiridion,* and in chapter 21 of his *City of God,* both of which are readily available in more than one English translation.

11

IS THERE LIFE AFTER DEATH?

Ronald F. Thiemann

My parents, both of whom lived into their eighties and shared more than sixty years of their lives together, died within nine months of each other. Their deaths provided a tragic parenthesis surrounding the 1994–95 academic year. My father's funeral was held on the day of Harvard Divinity School's opening fall convocation, and my mother's coincided with the following spring's commencement ceremonies. I was struck by the ironic concurrence of the academic calendar's rhythm with that of their passing away. It was almost as if these two modestly educated (they both ended formal education following elementary school) but experience-wise parents were reminding their theologian son of life's genuine priorities.

Some months before my father's death from lung and brain cancer, he underwent delicate surgery for repair of an abdominal aneurysm. The procedure was necessary to alleviate the severe stomach pain he was experiencing, but it also posed a significant risk of death in the operating room. He was clearly prepared for either outcome. I remember vividly my first visit with him following the successful surgery. While he was pleased that the pain had subsided, he was clearly disappointed that he had survived the operation. His own father had died when my dad was only two years old, and he had fervently hoped that his death would reunite them: "I wanted so much to see my father and to catch up on all I had missed." And then with an impish smile this lifelong Roman Catholic told his Lutheran son, "And I also wanted to get together with John XXIII and Martin Luther to see if they really had any serious disagreements."

I did not know how to respond to the stark and simple realism of my father's postmortem expectations. While I was touched by the innocence of his anticipation, I was quite skeptical of its theological soundness. Fortunately I had the good sense simply to listen to his remarkable statement of faith and to resist my instinctive desire to engage in critique. Still I could not share his naive confidence in the possibility of such afterlife conversations.

My mother's death from emphysema and heart failure was, as such deaths tend to be, a long and drawn-out affair. During the preceding nine months she had been hospitalized many times, and I had made several trips back to the Midwest to see her. When my brother called me the week before commencement to say that the doctors believed she would not live through the week, my first reaction was one of irritation. Not surprising, I thought to myself, that my mother, well known for her imperious demands, would now convene a dramatic deathbed farewell at the most inconvenient time of the year. Nonetheless, I decided to make the trek back to St. Louis, and I am forever grateful that I did. For not only was this to be a final farewell, but in sharing her dying with me she gave me one of the greatest gifts I have ever received.

My mother's last days were filled with long periods of sleep and semiconsciousness broken by brief but intense times of lucidity. During those precious periods we would talk together of childhood memories, or I would read to her from the books of poetry she so loved. Because she had refused all extraordinary care, she was blessedly free of the technological devices that create a physical barrier between the dying and those whom they love. Thus I could crawl into bed alongside her, and we could embrace until she fell again into sleep. These times gave us the opportunities to say those things we often think of saying but rarely do. So I thanked her for all she had given to me, particularly for the gift of learning to laugh at my own foibles. She responded by telling me that I was "the nearly perfect son." And, then, with the timing of a great comedian, she pushed me slightly away and said, "But, of course, I don't know what you do in your free time!" With that we collapsed into a fit of laughter that brought us both to tears. Soon thereafter she fell into a deep sleep, and though we had a few more brief conversations, never again would we share such a moment of intimacy.

What are we to make of such experiences? How are we to interpret my father's simple faith that he would be reunited with his father beyond the grave? How are we to understand my mother's ability to face death with life-affirming humor? Are these merely the naive acts of simple, uneducated folk, or do they possess a meaning that demands our more serious theological attention? If theology is, as the ancients declared, "faith seeking understanding," then how does faith's simplicity combine with the complexity of critical intellectual inquiry to yield genuine understanding? And how might theology help us to answer the everyday question, Is there life beyond the grave?

We live at a time of intense speculation about life after death. Research by physicians like Elisabeth Kübler-Ross has produced a vast literature describing and analyzing "near-death experiences." Participants in these studies often report "out-of-body episodes" in which they observe medical teams working to resuscitate their apparently lifeless corpses. Descriptions of being drawn to a bright light or sensations of deep calm and profound well-being are also commonplace. Popular depictions of communication between the spirits of the dead and their loved ones in movies like *Ghost* and *To Jillian on Her 37th Birthday* further fuel curiosity about the possibility and character of life beyond the grave.

While these phenomena may stimulate our imaginations, for Christians they do not provide either reliable information about the afterlife or a basis for our belief in life after death. Indeed, the Christian gospel proclaims that the belief in our own postgrave survival is grounded, not in any general claim about human beings at all, but in some very specific claims about Jesus of Nazareth. The fundamental witness of the Christian faith is that the destiny of humankind is inextricably tied to the destiny of Jesus.

The earliest Christian reflections on the afterlife are to be found in hymnic and other liturgical fragments embedded in the Epistles of the New Testament. They display the conviction that Christian teaching concerning resurrection involves the relation between Christ and the believer:

If you confess with your lips that Jesus is Lord and believe in your heart that God raised him from the dead, you will be saved. (Rom. 10:9)

But God, who is rich in mercy, out of the great love with which he loved us, even when we were dead through our trespasses, made us alive together with Christ (by grace you have been saved), and raised us up with him, and made us sit with him in the heavenly places in Christ Jesus. (Eph. 2:4–6)

You were buried with him [Christ] in baptism, in which you were also raised with him through faith in the working of God, who raised him from the dead. (Col. 2:12)

Through him [Christ] you have confidence in God, who raised him from the dead and gave him glory, so that your faith and hope are in God. (1 Pet. 1:21)

For Christians the question of whether we will experience life beyond the grave is inescapably tied to the question of whether Jesus, the crucified, now lives. For Christians the hope that we might experience life after death is grounded in the conviction that God has raised Jesus from the dead and so given us new life in him. Christian hope is thus grounded not in stories of near-death experiences or tales of spirits returning from the dead to communicate with the living. Christian hope is grounded always and only in the resurrection of Jesus from the dead.

> Now I would remind you, brethren, in what terms I preached to you the gospel, which you received, in which you stand, by which you are saved, if you hold it fast — unless you believed in vain.
> For I delivered to you as of first importance what I also received, that Christ died for our sins in accordance with the scriptures, that he was buried, that he was raised on the third day in accordance with the scriptures, and that he appeared to Cephas, then to the twelve. Then he appeared to more than five hundred brethren at one time, most of whom are still alive, though some have fallen asleep. Then he appeared to James, then to all the apostles. Last of all, as to one untimely born, he appeared also to me. (1 Cor. 15:1–8)

In these opening verses from 1 Corinthians 15, Saint Paul is quoting from an early Christian confession concerning Jesus' resurrection. Paul describes the gospel message as a form of "testimony," a tradition passed from one generation to the next: "the gospel, which you received, in which you stand, by

which you are saved." The declaration that Jesus the crucified now lives is part of the gospel message, the Good News
that in Jesus Christ a sinful and broken world has been reconciled to God. Jesus' resurrection is thus part of a larger
pattern of God's saving action designed to rescue humanity
from sin. Paul's gospel proclamation begins with the statement
"Christ died for our sins in accordance with the scriptures" to
remind his readers that the events of Jesus' death and resurrection are, not simple historical facts, but divine actions directed
toward *our* salvation. The gospel message thus describes the
drama by which God saves sinful humanity from the ultimate
consequences of our own sin, eternal death, that is, ultimate
separation from the creating and sustaining love of God. If we
hold fast to that which we have received, in which we stand,
and by which we are saved, then Jesus' destiny will become
our own.

Paul recounts the basic facts of this drama of salvation —
that Jesus died, was buried, and was raised on the third day —
and then focuses on the importance of Jesus' postresurrection
appearances to his followers. Most scholars believe that there
are two distinct traditions regarding Jesus' resurrection: the
earlier "appearance tradition" and the later "empty-tomb tradition." The earlier tradition emphasizes the reports of Jesus'
followers that they had seen and recognized him in the days
after his death. In addition to the appearances that Paul notes in
this passage, the Gospels report the memorable stories of Jesus'
appearances to Mary Magdalene, to the disciples hiding behind
closed doors, to Thomas, to Peter beside the Sea of Galilee, and
to the disciples on the way to Emmaus. In each of these cases
the followers witness to the continuity and identity between the
crucified and risen Lord. Initially the disciples fail to recognize
Jesus: Mary mistakes him for the gardener; the Emmaus disciples take him to be a stranger; Thomas refuses to believe the
disciples' report of Jesus' appearance; Peter and the other disciples fishing on the sea do not grasp that the man on the shore
is the risen Christ. But in every case Jesus engages in some familiar action that creates the startling recognition that the one
who stands before them is identical to the one they have seen
crucified:

Jesus said to her, "Mary." She turned and said to him in Hebrew, "Rab-boni!" (John 20:16)

When he was at table with them, he took the bread and blessed, and broke it, and gave it to them. And their eyes were opened and they recognized him. (Luke 24:30–31)

Then he said to Thomas, "Put your finger here, and see my hands; and put out your hand, and place it in my side; do not be faithless, but believing." Thomas answered him, "My Lord and my God!" (John 20:27–28)

He said to them, "Cast the net on the right side of the boat, and you will find some [fish]." So they cast it, and now they were not able to haul it in, for the quantity of fish. That disciple whom Jesus loved said to Peter, "It is the Lord!" (John 21:6–7)

These recognition stories are designed to show in narrative form the theological point made earlier by Paul, namely, that belief in Jesus' resurrection, and thus in one's own salvation, is a matter of faith not of sight: "Jesus said to him [Thomas], 'Have you believed because you have seen me? Blessed are those who have not seen and yet believe'" (John 20:29). Belief in the resurrection is not a matter of blind belief in a miraculous violation of the laws of nature. To confess that Jesus is risen from the dead is to assert that the almighty God, Creator of heaven and earth, has gained my salvation and that of the world through this remarkable act of loving-kindness. Thus Martin Luther in his *Small Catechism* can interpret the events of Jesus' life, death, and resurrection as intended by God for my personal salvation: "I believe that Jesus Christ, true God, begotten of the Father from eternity, and also true man, born of the Virgin Mary, is my Lord, who has redeemed me a lost and condemned creature, delivered me and freed me from all sins, from death, and from the power of the devil, not with silver and gold but with his holy and precious blood and his innocent sufferings and death." For Luther the challenge of faith is not only to believe that God in Christ has brought life out of death but to believe that he has done so *for my sake and for my salvation.*

Christ's resurrection is thus part of a larger Christian view of life in which all of reality is under the governing care of God's creating, sustaining, and reconciling love. To believe in

Christ's resurrection, and therefore in one's own, is to believe that God loves the world and all that is in it and so desires its ultimate reconciliation and salvation. It is a profound mistake to remove belief in resurrection from the larger pattern of belief about God's loving relationship to all that God has created. To focus simply on resurrection as a miracle that violates the laws of nature is to miss entirely the theological and spiritual meaning of the Christian gospel, namely, that the almighty and creative power that sustains the entire universe is in Christ "my God and my Lord," the one who knows me by name and loves me. To confess the resurrection of Christ is to make the audacious claim that the ultimate power of the universe is a loving God who brings life out of death and wills the ultimate reconciliation of the entire cosmos, including my own salvation. That confession flies in the face of the empirical observation that the world is "red in tooth and claw," a place of violence, suffering, and death. And yet that confession is essential to the Christian claim that Jesus the crucified now lives.

It is important to recognize, however, that the Christian gospel affirms both the reality of evil, suffering, and death and the greater reality of life's triumph over death, the victory of God's love over all that opposes it. In contrast to the many New Age philosophies that deny the reality of evil so that they may affirm the finality of love, the Christian gospel faces evil squarely and still announces the triumph of God's grace. That is why resurrection can never be separated from crucifixion, for the miracle of Easter can only be experienced by one who has stood at the foot of the cross. Jesus' appearances to his followers are so important because they provide the evidence that the same Jesus who lived, laughed, ate, and taught among them, but then suffered a cruel and agonizing death, now truly lives. That is why the stories emphasize that Jesus is finally recognized when he performs some everyday task like breaking the bread or speaking a name. Jesus is present to his disciples, not as some ephemeral spirit, but as the same embodied individual whom they had known and loved. The Christian faith confesses that life beyond the grave is in some sense embodied life, that is, life in which individual identity endures from death into life everlasting:

So is it with the resurrection of the dead. What is sown is perishable, what is raised is imperishable. It is sown in dishonor, it is raised in glory. It is sown in weakness, it is raised in power. It is sown a physical body, it is raised a spiritual body....

Lo! I tell you a mystery. We shall not all sleep, but we shall all be changed, in a moment, in the twinkling of an eye, at the last trumpet. For the trumpet will sound, and the dead will be raised imperishable, and we shall be changed. For this perishable nature must put on the imperishable, and this mortal nature must put on immortality. When the perishable puts on the imperishable, and the mortal puts on immortality, then shall come to pass the saying that is written:

> "Death is swallowed up in victory."
> "O death, where is thy victory?
> O death, where is thy sting?"

... But thanks be to God, who gives us the victory through our Lord Jesus Christ. (1 Cor. 15:42–43, 51–57)

This ultimate confession of Christian hope requires the language of poetry for its full expression, and yet it manifests the essential theological elements of the Christian understanding of life after death. For Christians life after death is embodied life, life in which one's personal identity endures on the other side of the grave. And yet the resurrected body is not merely an extension of the weak, diseased, and perishable body that precedes it. The resurrected body is, in Paul's intentionally paradoxical term, a "spiritual body," that is, a body that is recognizably my own and yet is now imperishable and immortal. The Gospel writers capture this same sense in their descriptions of Jesus' body in the postresurrection appearances. When the disciples at Emmaus finally recognize Jesus in the breaking of bread, "he vanished out of their sight" (Luke 24:31). When Jesus first appears to the disciples, "the doors being shut where the disciples were ... Jesus came and stood among them and ... showed them his hands and his side" (John 20:20). Jesus is embodied, and yet his bodily presence is different: he appears and vanishes without the usual human restraints. In this fashion the Gospel writers seek to communicate the postresurrection reality that Paul identifies as a "spiritual body." Jesus' body is the one that underwent suffering and death, for it carries within it the wounds from the nails and the spear. And yet this same body has now taken on imperishable form because God has raised it up to life everlasting. There is no denial of death in the Christian gospel; rather, death has been swallowed up in victory, and its sting has been forever removed. That is the witness and the hope of the Christian understanding of life after death.

The theologian cannot fully explain why or how persons come to believe the witness and promise of the Christian gospel. The ultimate explanation of that mysterious movement from unbelief to faith lies beyond the theologian's competence. But we can say that those who believe that Jesus the crucified now lives, and therefore believe that their own salvation has been secured, have rightly understood the meaning of the gospel's promise. Those who by faith do believe this witness are then asked to exemplify the theological virtues of faith, love, and hope in all that they do. To believe the Christian gospel is to enter into a life of discipleship, following the crucified and risen Christ. Such discipleship calls the followers to a ministry in behalf of those to whom Christ ministered — the poor, the outcasts, those on the margins of society. The way of the cross passes through urban ghettos and rural wastelands, through hospital rooms of the incurably ill and dying, through those deep corridors of despair within the hearts of those who are victims of violence or abuse. Followers of the Crucified are called to identify with those who suffer, but as they do, they are also called to proclaim the good news that the Crucified has risen, that suffering and despair are not the final judgment upon God's creation. Those who enter the life of discipleship are thus called to exemplify a "cruciform hope" within a world too often plagued by despair and cynicism.

Even if some are willing to affirm the message of the Christian gospel that the Crucified now lives and thereby enter into the life of discipleship, doesn't resurrection faith require of them a sacrifice of the intellect? Does resurrection faith demand belief in corpses come back to life and in ghostly appearances of those who have died? In this light doesn't resurrection faith look suspiciously like the New Age pieties mentioned? Can robust Christian faith in the resurrection coexist with serious rational inquiry?

The challenge that the Christian gospel presents to all who

encounter it is to believe that the almighty Creator of the universe is a personal and loving God who through the death and resurrection of Jesus has conquered death and thereby won my salvation and the reconciliation of the world. For the earliest Christian community this belief required the assertion of the continuity of Jesus' identity before and after his death by crucifixion. Paul's language of the "spiritual body" and the Gospel writers' accounts of the "appearances" are attempts to express this continuity of identity in imaginative poetic language and vivid narrative depiction. This language is the means by which the basic truth of the continued embodied existence beyond the grave of Jesus and believers is communicated and affirmed. The claim that Jesus the crucified now lives and that I, too, will live with him in continuity with my earlier bodily identity is the heart of the distinctive Christian witness regarding life after death. The linguistic means by which this fundamental claim is expressed will always be partial and incomplete because human language can never fully communicate the reality of God's saving act of bringing life out of the despairing depths of the grave. Even the biblical language itself will be inadequate in face of the extraordinary mystery of the resurrection.

Still the question remains, does resurrection faith commit one to belief in the miraculous resuscitation of corpses or the unexpected appearance of apparitions? It is important to stress that Christian teaching requires belief in only two instances of resurrection, that of Jesus and that of the dead on the last day. It is precisely the *uniqueness* of these two events that the Christian gospel affirms. Consequently, belief in the resurrection in no way implies a general belief in miraculous resuscitation or communication between the spirits of the dead and the living. Indeed, if Christian belief in the resurrection is thought to be an instance of these latter beliefs, then its basic meaning is misunderstood and trivialized. Christians confess that Jesus' resurrection is a miracle, that is, an overturning of our ordinary beliefs about the finality of death, but they do so only because they affirm the truth of the larger story concerning God's redemptive and reconciling love of which the resurrection is one essential part. The Christian faith does not demand a general belief in miracles, only the belief that God's love is capable of bringing life out of death. Or to put it another way, Christians believe in the miraculous power of resurrection because they believe the gospel.

"For now we see in a glass darkly, but then face to face. Now I know in part; then I shall understand fully, even as I have been fully understood" (1 Cor. 13:12). As I reflect on my parents' witness of faith as they faced their own dying, I realize that their confidence was grounded in their simple, but not naive, trust in the message of the gospel. Being assured that Jesus had been raised from the dead, they fully expected that they, too, would be raised to everlasting life. I do not know whether spiritual bodies communicate with one another in the way my father expected, but I do know that his hope was consistent with Christian belief in the enduring personal identity of resurrected bodies. I also know that my mother's sense of humor in the face of her own painful death was a remarkable witness to a gospel faith that can acknowledge the reality of death and still delight in the good things of a world created and redeemed by a loving God. Though we undoubtedly differ in the way we express our faith, we share — and will continue to share in the eternity of God's love — a common hope in our own resurrection from the dead. And it is that hope in the resurrection that defines the distinctive Christian understanding of life after death.

For Further Reading

Bynum, Caroline Walker. *The Resurrection of the Body.* New York: Columbia University Press, 1995. The most thorough and readable study of the history of Christian thought on the resurrection of the body.

Davis, Stephen T., Kendall, Daniel and O'Collins, Gerald, eds. *The Resurrection: An Interdisciplinary Symposium on the Resurrection of Jesus.* New York: Oxford University Press, 1997. An interesting set of essays by biblical scholars, historians, theologians, and philosophers on the meaning and significance of resurrection for Christian faith.

First Corinthians 15. This is Paul's classic statement of resurrection faith.